The Transforming Cross

CHARLES S. McCOY &
MARJORIE CASEBIER McCOY

The Transforming Cross

Abingdon / Nashville

The Transforming Cross

Copyright © 1977 by Abingdon

Library of Congress Cataloging in Publication Data
MCCOY, CHARLES S
The Transforming cross.
Bibliography: p.
1. Jesus Christ—Seven last words. I. McCoy, Marjorie Casebier,
1934-   joint author. II. Title. BT456.M25   232.9'635   77-
10884
ISBN 0-687-42507-7

Quotation on pages 93-94 is from Patricia Vought Schneider's *Peter*,
published by Baker's Plays, Boston, MA 02111. Poem "Mea Culpa" from
Oh, I See (pp. 84-85), published by the Friends of Helen Berryhill, is
reprinted by permission of Susan Berryhill. Quotation on pages 74-75
from *The Angel That Troubled the Waters, and Other Plays* by Thornton
N. Wilder, copyright Union Trust Company, executor and trustee under
the last will and testament of Thornton N. Wilder, is used with their
permission. Excerpts on pages 43-44, from *The Man Born to Be King* by
Dorothy L. Sayers, copyright 1943 by Dorothy L. Sayers are reprinted
with permission of Harper & Row, Publishers, Inc., and Gollanez.

Scripture quotations noted RSV are taken from the Revised Standard
Version Common Bible, copyright © 1973.

MANUFACTURED BY THE PARTHENON PRESS AT
NASHVILLE, TENNESSEE, UNITED STATES OF AMERICA

Dedicated with appreciation
for their early influence on us
to Charles and Dorcas Jones
and
Eugene and Marian Muench,
whose lives tell the story of our faith.

Contents

Preface

I. **Dwelling In**

Remembering the Story of Our Faith **15**

II. **Listening To**

Seven Last Words from the Cross **25**

1. Forgiveness:
Estrangement Transformed into Presence **30**
2. Redemption:
Helplessness Transformed into Hope **40**
3. Comfort:
Pain Transformed into Action **49**
4. Loneliness:
Despair Transformed into Faith **58**
5. Suffering:
Need Transformed into Love **67**
6. Fulfillment:
Failure Transformed into Wholeness **77**
7. Trust: Death Transformed into Life **86**

III. **Breaking Out**

Transforming Human Living **99**

Bibliography **109**

Preface

Countless paintings, poems, and books have been inspired by the Cross of Jesus Christ. Even more important are the human lives lived in faith and hope and love through the power emanating from that hill outside Jerusalem.

This book takes its place as a continuation of that long tradition. In writing it, we have drawn on many sources—persons, works of art, ideas—to focus on the seven brief statements spoken from the cross and to testify to the continuing presence of Jesus in our own lives and in the world today. Clearly, the most important source is Jesus as we encounter him in the Gospels and through the heritage of Christian faith into which we were long ago inducted.

Another influence upon us has been the lifelong context of family and friends whose lives have told us the story of our faith. Teachers in church, in college, in seminary, and in university have helped us grasp the depth and height of that story. Further understanding has come through the communities of Pacific School of Religion and Trinity United Methodist Church in Berkeley, where week by week we join in worship and work with others to live in the grace and power of the Cross. With gratitude we acknowledge all these sources.

In particular, there are persons to whom we are especially indebted. First, there are two teachers and friends, now dead, who inspired the framework of what follows—H. Richard Niebuhr (1894-1962) and Michael Polanyi (1891-1976). Those familiar with the works of these two seminal minds will recognize the importance of their writings for our approach. Second, there is Jürgen Moltmann, friend and colleague, who continues to remind us in his life and in his writings of the close relationship between faith, social justice, and human liberation. Third, Thornton Wilder, Frederick Buechner, and Elizabeth Berryhill have taught us what it means to dwell in the story of our faith with loyalty illumined by dramatic artistry. They have given us the confidence to treat the events of Jesus' Passion as a drama involving real people, without pretending that we have entered the minds of persons from an era long past.

Throughout the book we have sought to use inclusive language, a task easily accomplished within our own text. The undertaking became more difficult when we wanted to use material from other people who wrote prior to current awareness of the need to broaden the gender implications of language. In quoting ancient or contemporary sources, we looked for passages that are in harmony with the standard of inclusiveness, but in a few places we use excerpts whose power and meaning seem to us to transcend the limits of particular words.

Much of our biblical material is taken from the Revised Standard Version of the Bible and is so indicated. In places where we wanted to avoid the gender limitations of RSV language, and where we wished to suggest new dimensions of meaning in familiar passages, we paraphrased the RSV or developed a different version by drawing on several translations. We believe this effort is part of the tradition that calls people in all ages to wrestle with new ways to understand the story of our faith.

We are grateful to Pacific School of Religion for sabbatic leave and to Fred and Millie Twining, close friends and co-workers, for the use of their cabin in Inverness, California, as a place to write. With this time and quiet space we have been able to bring together these reflections on the seven words from the cross.

I
Dwelling In

In the beginning was the Faithful Action, and the Faithful Action was with God, and the Faithful Action was God. . . . And the Faithful Action became flesh and dwelt among us.

—*John 1:1, 14*

Remembering
the Story of Our Faith

Now I want you to remember the Good News that I proclaimed to you, which you accepted, and in which your faith is firmly rooted. That is the gospel through which you are saved, if you hold it strongly in memory—unless you have believed for naught. For I passed on to you what is most important in that which I also accepted: that Christ died for our sins as scripture tells us; that Christ was buried and raised to life again in three days as scripture tells us; and that Peter saw him and then all twelve apostles, and later more than five hundred disciples, most of whom are still alive. After that he appeared to James and to all the apostles. And last of all, he appeared to me; and I experienced the strange power of new birth.

—I Corinthians 14:1-8

Whenever we speak of what we believe most deeply, we do not write books of theology or philosophy. Instead

15

we tell the stories of our faith. In the Christian community we tell the old, old story passed down to us in the Bible about God dwelling in humanity, and about the fulfillment of life that comes through the supreme discovery that we dwell in God. In telling this story, we testify to the highest truth that has possessed us.

The center of the story of our faith is Jesus Christ. We tell of his birth of humble parentage in a stable, and we sing this part of the story in joyful carols that even the little children know and love. We tell of his life of teaching, healing, and empowering among the multitudes. Our story reaches its climax as he wrestles in the garden with a terrible destiny, suffers a shameful, incredibly painful death, and emerges from the grave in glorious resurrection.

Jesus Christ is the center of our story. But Jesus points beyond himself. He is the faithful action at the heart of creation who is now dwelling among us. Jesus points to the larger reality of God who makes covenant with the world and its people. The story of Jesus proclaims the unfolding drama of God's continuing action in history, of God's faithful love, of God's promises and the fulfillment of them. God's faithful action creates the world, judges our sin, and through transforming love reconciles and renews humanity and the whole creation.

In order to remember the entire story of our faith, we tell of the Hebrew tribes becoming captive in Egypt, of their exodus under the leadership of Moses, and of the covenant of blessing and liberation that Yahweh makes with them. Jesus is the new Moses through whom the bonds of captivity to sin are loosed and humanity offered continuing exodus from alienation and despair. Our story includes accounts of repeated human rebellion against God and human unfaithfulness to the covenant. We tell of the prophets' denunciation of sin and their proclamation of God's unfailing faithfulness to the covenant and its promises. The Lord's Supper is a reenactment of covenant-making, a remembering that God continues the covenant in Jesus Christ, and—as we participate in communion—a renewing of our unsteady loyalty to that covenant. Paul remembers and tells us this part of the story:

> For I received from the Lord what I also delivered to you, that the Lord Jesus on the night when he was betrayed took bread, and when he had given thanks, he broke it, and said, "This is my body which is broken for you. Do this in remembrance of me." In the same way also the cup, after supper, saying, "This cup is the new covenant in my blood. Do this, as often as you drink it, in remembrance of me." For as often as you eat this bread and drink the cup, you proclaim the Lord's death until he comes. (I Cor. 11:23-26 RSV)

With Jesus as center and focus, the story of our faith is enlarged to include the entire human experience. It goes back to the creation of the world and moves forward to embrace the human weakness and greatness of David, the call to social justice in the prophets, and the understanding of faith forged and refined in the fires of failure, catastrophe, and exile. Through the story of Israel in the Old Testament, we are prepared for and enabled to understand Jesus as Messiah, as the Christ, in the New Testament. As Christians we must tell the whole story of our faith in order to grasp any part of it.

We tell the story also of the community that came to believe in Jesus as the Messiah, as the Anointed of God who redeems humanity. In a world ruled by Rome, the early Christians came to trust in Jesus Christ and to proclaim their faith to people sated with too many religions, to powers hostile to the Way and bent upon exterminating its followers. The small Christian community endured persecution, performed acts of great courage and heroism, grew with amazing rapidity, and eventually triumphed over the power of the Roman Empire. Much of the Christian story in those first three centuries is written in the blood of martyrs, whose incandescent deeds command our continuing devotion.

But worldly victory had more perils for Christian faith than did persecution. The church triumphant on earth became powerful, wealthy, and cruel, repeating the sins of pride and rebellion as old as Israel and Adam. Even so, the story of Jesus continued to be told and continued to awaken repentance and faith.

As we remember the story of God's faithful action coming to dwell in humanity, as we come to dwell in that story by telling it to one another, we discover ourselves dwelling together in Jesus Christ and he in us. His story becomes our story. The faithful action of God we encounter in the story of Jesus becomes the sovereign reality that we meet in all events, in all relations, in all history.

In one way, remembering our faith by telling it in story does no more than testify to the power of saga and dramatic recital in human communities. Children love stories and can be engaged no more deeply or for a longer time than by a vivid tale told well. We have forgotten most of what happened to us as children, but we remember stories told or read to us in the warm context of love. Our first knowledge of Christianity, after the wordless actions of caring love, probably came from Bible stories about Jesus, about Joseph's coat of many colors, about the call to the boy Samuel, and about the heroic death of Stephen. When H. Richard Niebuhr reminds us that "the preaching of the early Christian church . . . was primarily a simple recital of the great events connected with the historical appearance of Jesus Christ and a confession of what had happened to the community of disciples," he is pointing to one characteristic of the message that continues to be a source of its power (16.43).*

As Christians, we tell the story of Jesus Christ not as remote past but, as present event, in order that what happened then may be with us now and enable us to live today in the promises of God and toward a future filled with life and hope. The story of our faith becomes the means by which we tell each other what life and death, God and humanity, and our responsibilities to one another really are.

When as Christians we gather, we witness to our faith by telling the story—by singing the story of Jesus Christ and dwelling in God's faithful action become flesh as the reality in which we live. In the poignant events of our recital, we come to know ourselves as participants in that

---

*Throughout, a two-digit system of references will be used. The first number shows the source as listed in the Bibliography; the second refers to the page of that source on which the quotation appears.

drama of tragedy and triumph. It is our story, our own faith, our very own life.

We call each person who reads or hears these words to dwell in the story of Jesus Christ. Then you will discover the transforming power of the Cross. You will know that the message of Christian faith is addressed to you. Biblical witness is not a cold telling of distant facts but a response to the sovereign reality revealed in Jesus Christ and a call to others to join in that response of faith. The New Testament writers, Walter Wink tells us, "bore witness to events which led them to faith. They wrote 'from faith to faith,' to evoke or augment faith in their readers" (28.2). In these pages, we too are writing from faith to faith. We invite you to study what Jesus said from the cross, not to enjoy a good, even a superb, story, but in order that together we may come to dwell more fully in the reality of God to which the story directs us, so that the transforming power of the Cross may change us and our world.

During the time leading up to Easter, during Lent and on Good Friday, the storytelling character of Christian faith, the recital of our history, becomes even more direct and vivid than usual. In the presence of God—to the glory of God—we focus on the events that set the Christian movement loose in the world: the condemnation of Jesus by Roman authorities, his humiliation at the hands of the crowd and the soldiers, his suffering on the cross, his death and burial, and the new beginning for the world and for us in his resurrection.

More than any other single occurrence, it is the Cross that has remained the enduring, magnetic center of the

Christian drama. As D. M. Baillie suggests in *God Was in Christ:* "The most remarkable fact in the whole history of religious thought is this: that when the early Christians looked back and pondered on the dreadful thing that had happened, it made them think of the redeeming love of God. Not simply of the love of Jesus, but of the love of God" (1.184). Here in the crucifixion the meaning of God's faithful action in Jesus Christ becomes clear. Around the Cross we learn who we are, who are the neighbors we are commanded to love, what is the hope to which we are called, and what this tangled world is all about.

In the story of their faith, the Hebrews of the Old Testament stand on the banks of the river Jordan. They remember the past in which God delivered them from bondage and made covenant with them. And they look forward toward Canaan in the hope that God is leading them into a future filled with promise.

In the same way, Christians stand always at the Cross. We remember the promises of the covenant for continuing liberation from the many forms of bondage that enslave us. In the presence of the Crucified One upon the cross, we look around us in perplexity at the loneliness and forsakenness, the suffering and guilt, the cruelty and injustice rampant in our world. And with hearts illumined by faith, we look forward in hope through the dimness of mystery to the fulfillment of God's promises in resurrection and the final power of love. To faith, Jürgen Moltmann writes, "The world is full of all kinds of possibilities, namely all the possibilities of the God of hope. It sees reality and mankind in the hand of him whose voice calls into history from its end, saying, 'Behold, I make all things new,' and from hearing this word of promise it acquires the freedom to renew life here and to change the face of the world" (14.26).

With faith in the hope given by God's love, Christians live always in the presence of the transforming Cross of Jesus Christ.

II
Listening To

When evening came, Jesus had supper with the Twelve. He said to them as they were eating, "I tell you truly, one among you will betray me." At this, all of them were distressed and one after another began saying to him, "Lord, is it I?"
—Matthew 26:20-22

Seven Last
Words from the Cross

Then the soldiers of the governor took Jesus into the praetorium, and they gathered the whole battalion before him. And they stripped him and put a scarlet robe upon him, and plaiting a crown of thorns they put it on his head, and put a reed in his right hand. And kneeling before him they mocked him, saying, "Hail, King of the Jews!" And they spat upon him, and took the reed and struck him on the head. And when they had mocked him, they stripped him of the robe, and put his own clothes on him, and led him away to crucify him.

As they went out, they came upon a man of Cyrene, Simon by name; this man they compelled to carry his cross. And when they came to place called Golgotha (which means the place of a skull), they offered him wine to drink, mingled with gall; but when he tasted it, he would not drink it. And when they had crucified him, they divided his garments among them by casting lots; then they sat down and kept watch over him there.

—Matthew 27:27-36 RSV

When we dwell in the story of our faith so fully that it becomes the story of our own life, we listen to it with our entire attention. Not only do we pray without ceasing so that all our actions strive to become responses to God the Faithful One, but we also listen without ceasing so that the story of Jesus Christ becomes the meaning of everything that happens to us. Only as we listen in this way do our ears become capable of real hearing.

Listening and hearing in this way means that we place ourselves within the story and recognize ourselves as characters in the drama being enacted around Jesus. We join the disciples at the Last Supper. We fail to watch with Jesus in the Garden. We are with Peter—we *are* Peter—as he denies his Lord. We follow fearfully from afar and witness at a cowardly distance the events at Pilate's court and on Golgotha.

In his great *St. Matthew Passion,* Johann Sebastian Bach catches this sense of contemporaneity and identification with the events of Jesus' last days. Following the account in Matthew's Gospel, Bach has Jesus sing the accusation, "One of you will betray me." And all the disciples respond together, "Lord, is it I, is it I?" So must all Christians discover themselves present as Jesus foretells betrayal, and ask from the depth of their being, knowing it is so, "Lord, is it I?"

When we dwell in the story of Jesus Christ, we listen to the narrative as present in the midst of it and hear the words of Jesus addressed to us—because they are! And in being addressed to us, the words and actions of Jesus have the power to penetrate to the heart of our being and transform us. "Were you there when they crucified my Lord?" the spiritual asks, and in our mind's eye we see ourselves trembling on Calvary. "Beneath the cross of Jesus I fain would take my stand," we sing, and as our lips form the words, the shadow of that cross falls across our lives.

Elizabeth Berryhill, commenting on Tennessee Williams' *Glass Menagerie,* illumines this striking characteristic of dramatic action. "Drama," she says, "is a means of revelation. It is a way to uncover that which is normally covered, to open that which is normally closed. Drama has the power to penetrate the secret lives of people, going behind the scenes, behind the way things appear to themselves and to others. Drama goes beneath the surface into the reality of things—exposing the truth" (3.66). And, in so doing, it changes those whom it touches.

The story of the crucifixion must be pieced together from the Four Gospels. John reports that Jesus had to carry his own cross, but Matthew, Mark, and Luke all say that he had help from Simon of Cyrene. Simon was a chance visitor in the city, a passerby, Mark calls him, whom the soldiers compelled to bear the heavy cross. But the accidental encounter apparently changed the world for Simon. Mark identifies Simon as the father of Alexander and Rufus. In his letter to the church at Rome, Paul writes, "Greet Rufus, eminent in the Lord, also his mother and mine" (Rom. 16:13 RSV). For Simon, who only felt the weight of the cross upon his shoulder and saw Jesus nailed to it, that piece of wood became the transforming Cross.

All four Evangelists agree that the terrible event of crucifixion took place at Golgotha, the place of the Skull. It was most probably a familiar site for the execution of criminals, located just outside the city walls of Jerusalem.

The Gospels do not tell us exactly how Jesus was crucified. Details of such an execution were evidently so well known in that day that no complete description was necessary. As nearly as can be ascertained, crucifixion was carried out by nailing the victim to two crossed pieces of wood, feet to one, hands stretched out as far as possible to the other. When the cross was dropped upright into a hole to keep it in place, the person hung upon it, held there by the spikes. It was among the slowest, most painful, cruelest forms of death inflicted even in the harsh world of ancient despotism. A crucified person apparently did not die through loss of blood but from asphyxiation, as the muscles of the abdomen contracted in the vain attempt to hold the body upright and diminish the excruciating pain. It was a death carefully designed to be filled with agony and suffering. No wonder Jesus' executioners, perhaps from some vestige of human sympathy, offered him something to drink that might have deadened the pain a little. But according to Matthew and Mark, he refused it. This was the way Jesus approached his death.

According to the accounts given us in the Gospels, Jesus made seven brief statements while hanging on the cross. These seven last "words" are not the same in any two of the versions. Once again, we must put the story together from several sources. The total of seven words is derived from the statements of all four reports. In the way the words have been put in order, they reveal the inner journey Jesus travels as he is dying on the cross.

For Christians, these last words of Jesus have always had special, enduring meaning. That they were remembered, passed on carefully in the oral tradition of stories told again and again in the Christian community, and at last set down in the Gospels testifies to the way in which they have been treasured. Recorded in scripture, woven into the events as described by the Evangelists, these seven utterances have been engraved on the heart of the Christian movement. As believers have dwelt in them, listened to them with eager hearts, meditated upon them, their meaning has been extended and enriched through the centuries for all who have shared in the life-transforming power of Christian faith.

Through these seven words, the significance of the Cross of Jesus Christ is disclosed in diverse and striking ways. Here Jesus, believed in as the enfleshment of the Divine Reality at the core of the world, addresses the persons around him—and the Creator as well—as the moment of supreme crisis and greatest fulfillment of his destiny as faithful action. We can with the aid of these statements come to understand God and the dealings of God with humanity with a depth and clarity provided seldom if ever elsewhere in scripture or in the tradition of the church.

In the seven words from the cross, God addresses us as human beings. The words speak to us of mercy and forgiveness. They speak to us of alienation, loneliness, and despair. They speak of God's compassion for human trials. The words speak of hope beyond tragedy. And most of all, they speak of the great price of divine suffering which is offered for the renewal of humanity and the re-creation of history.

Jesus said, "And I, in being lifted up from the earth, will draw all people to me" (John 12:32). At the place of the Skull, called Calvary, we see Christ lifted up before our eyes, and we are called to faith in God through the loving, faithful action there. Christ's seven last words offer us in unforgettable form the story of our faith. As we dwell in that story with their aid and listen again to what Jesus says to us, we may find the power by which human life, our human life, is being transformed.

1. Forgiveness:
Estrangement Transformed into Presence

"My God, forgive them; for they do not know what they are doing."

—*Luke 23:34*

At Golgotha the Roman soldiers carry out their assignment. They strip Jesus' clothes from him and lay him out on the crosspieces. Some hold him while others drive spikes through his hands and feet into the wood. They lift the cross with Jesus nailed to it and let it drop into the hole dug for it in the ground. Flesh pulls abruptly and harshly, but the spikes hold with excruciating firmness. And so the searing pain of crucifixion begins.

Jesus is lifted up in cruel humiliation for all to see—betrayed by one of his followers and deserted by almost all the rest, tried by authorities who feared that he threatened their power, sentenced to death by a ruler who would not resist a mob, mocked by mercenaries, nailed to a crosstree by indifferent executioners.

What a fate for the teacher who spoke of love! Surely the hard realities of the place of the Skull must end such sentimentality. Yet, Luke tells us, the first words Jesus speaks from the cross convey a message of forgiveness: "My God, forgive them; for they do not know what they are doing."

From birth to resurrection, as the drama of Jesus' life unfolds before us, the unexpected happens again and again. The ordinary becomes extraordinary as the touch of Jesus reveals unanticipated meaning. Dwelling in the story of God's faithful action enfleshed in Jesus, we see it is filled with surprise, even paradox. The sovereign power of creation is revealed through the birth of a baby in a manger. At twelve years of age Jesus astonishes his parents by staying behind in the temple in Jerusalem and amazes the teachers there with his understanding. When he returns to Nazareth from the wilderness, he shocks the worshipers at his hometown synagogue by proclaiming a message of healing and liberation and by placing himself in the line of prophets.

Jesus eats with tax collectors and sinners—we did not expect that from the Son of God. He drives money changers from the temple—we did not expect that from the Prince of Peace. He rides into Jerusalem on a donkey, scarcely what we expect from the Savior of the world. That the Almighty dwelling in human flesh submits to humiliation and crucifixion confounds our logic. And the resurrection contradicts our most reliable experience of the natural order.

But all these elements of the Christian story are in many ways no more astounding than the reversal of human nature that takes place from the cross. Now, nearing his death, unjustly condemned, hanging there in agony, Jesus speaks words, not of bitterness, but of forgiveness—we certainly did not expect that!

What are we to make of this act of forgiveness? What does it mean for Christian faith and life? What does it mean for us?

Jesus' word of forgiveness speaks most decisively to our sin and estrangement. There would be no need to talk of forgiveness to the soldiers or to us were not humanity alienated from God by our sin. From the Godward side, Jesus on the cross is estranged from everyone around him. His disciples are disillusioned and bewildered by what has happened; they have withdrawn to a safe distance, fearful lest identification with their teacher endanger their lives. The crowd that demanded his crucifixion is vindictive and curious. The women who weep for him are rebuked and do not understand what is happening. Jesus' silence and vulnerability bring out the worst in the Roman soldiers, who mock him and gamble for his garments. The thieves crucified with him deserve their punishment and know it. Though Jesus is physically close to all these people who are part of the Passion story, between him and every one of them there is a gaping chasm.

As we seek to take our place within the drama of Jesus' trial and execution, we find ourselves also estranged. Though we would be close to him in faith, we are distant, most obviously, in time. But the more we overcome this separation by remembering the events of the Cross as the story of our faith and dwelling in these happenings as the story of our own life, the more a different kind of separation and estrangement becomes clear to us. There on Calvary we discover that we are sinners in need of repentance.

We are as close to Christ as the disciple who betrayed him. Judas Iscariot placed great hope in Jesus. He looked to Jesus to lead a glorious revolution that would drive the legions of Rome from Jerusalem and establish the reign of God. When his expectations were disappointed finally by Jesus' firm rejection of violent revolution, Judas turned away from him and sold out. How close we still are to Judas! Some of us continue to look to Jesus as leader of violent revolution rather than as manifestation of that power which is revolutionizing human consciousness and history. And others of us want God to bring us success and happiness, and we intend to have our way—or find within ourselves the Judas who betrays his Lord. How difficult it is for us to repent, to turn from our own willfulness and pray with Jesus in Gethsemane, "Not my will, but thine!" We are as close to the Cross as Judas, and as distant.

We are as close to Jesus as the chief priests and scribes. We have no objection to the meek and mild teacher of love. He may be a good influence on our children. He may discourage crime in the streets. But if he endangers our power or requires any sacrifice of us, if he threatens our bank account or our national security, we turn swiftly against him.

We are as close to Jesus as Peter. We are willing to declare our loyalty to him when he delivers to us the keys of heaven. But when he stand condemned and rejected by the powers of society, we deny we ever knew him.

We are as close to him as the mob that cried, "Crucify him! Crucify him!" Ready to jump on the bandwagon of those who welcomed Jesus into Jerusalem, we stay with the crowd when it demands his death. Such outbursts of mob hysteria by people like us have tortured and oppressed the innocent throughout human history—the rush to condemn heretics in the Inquisition, the witch trials in Salem, the political witch hunts of the Committee on Un-American Activities, and the detention camps for Japanese Americans in World War II. How difficult it is to resist the pressures of the crowd. We are as close to Christ as the Jerusalem mob that demanded his execution, and just as distant from his spirit.

We are as close to Jesus as was Pilate, that figure of power who saw no fault in Jesus but feared the political impact of an aroused public. How like Pilate we are today! Our political leaders conform to the latest opinion poll. Afraid of losing face or social position, we alter our standards the way the chameleon takes on the color of its surroundings. Too many Christians took no part in the struggle for equal treatment of minorities when it was dangeous. Few joined the opposition to the Vietnam "war" until public sentiment shifted against it. Lacking the courage of the Cross, we wash our hands of hard decisions and step back with Pilate to watch Jesus suffer—across the chasm created by our own cowardice.

We are close to the Cross and yet far away. When we gaze upward at the Divine Goodness stretching toward eternity, we know that we are distant in guilt and in shame from the Faithful One who suffers there.

Then comes the astonishing surprise. Our estrangement from God is not the final word. Into the void of human sin, Jesus speaks to us (Roman soldiers all, with mallets and nails still in our hands) the words of forgiveness: "My God, forgive them; for they do not know what they are doing."

Indeed, when it comes to our participation in the world's inhumanities, we usually do not know. Blinded by ambition, pride, self-righteous passions, fear, greed—our vision limited by social pressure and "group-think"—we fail to see very far ahead. Lost in the human jungle, we miss the best part of living. In trying to save the investment we have in our little selves, our society, and our world, we overlook the larger possibilities and run the risk of blowing the whole shebang. As individuals we exchange the possibilities of human respect and love for hatred and isolation. In society we throw away justice and dignity among social groups in favor of discrimination, animosity, and crime born of poverty and frustration. Throughout the world we discard peace and mutual aid and replace them with national pride, nuclear threats, and mass starvation.

This is no way to live. When we reject the love of God in order to satisfy our frenzy to accumulate unjust and excessive wealth or to flaunt our national superiority, we not only run the risk of destruction, we also miss out on truly abundant living. Quite literally, we do not know what we are doing.

In asking God to forgive those crucifying him, Jesus opens the door to their potential for awareness. Noting Paul Ricoeur's observation that "a genuine fault is a hidden fault, and it requires an external revealer," Paul Tournier suggests:

This revealer is the Word of God, the Word which addresses us through the Bible and the Church by the voices of the prophets, through the word and example of Christ, and by the message of the Apostles; sometimes through the mouth of a friend, by some test or blessing, by some humiliating or pleasant circumstance. But it always leads to an awakening of conscience and to the uncovering of some hidden guilt. (25.172)

Perhaps the hearts of the centurions were touched by this first word of Jesus so that later they were led to reflect on their actions and realize what they had done, a first step toward repentance and reconciliation.

The forgiveness from the cross, therefore, not only discloses our alienation from one another and from God, it also reveals the possibility of transformation. On Calvary Jesus asks forgiveness for his tormentors and thereby changes estrangement from them into living presence. He takes our sin upon himself and transforms our guilt into repentance. He does for us what we cannot do for ourselves—he forgives us in God. His words spoken through the deed of suffering love are for us the outstretched hands of God. "In spite of everything you are, in spite of everything you have said and done," God says to us, "come to me." The chasm between God and us is changed into a deep and powerful presence together in Jesus Christ.

To know ourselves as forgiven does not eliminate the past or undo the unfolding consequences of human misdeeds. But forgiveness does transform our past, our present, and our future, freeing us from bondage to our old ways. No longer are we gripped by a paralyzing remorse for the past. Our guilt is overcome and we may live, not as though our misdeeds have been erased, but without their weight dragging us down.

At times we experience this cleansing power of forgiveness in personal relations. A rift with a friend occurs. A yawning chasm opens between us, hurting each of us. We still visit and converse, but the old relation is gone. Estrangement chills every word every attempt to touch. The surface closeness only accentuates the distance. We may even avoid each other in order to evade the pain. Then, out of the suffering and a deeper love, one of us finds the courage to say, "I'm sorry," and the other responds, "Oh, no, it was really my fault. Forgive me." A bridge is thrown across the abyss. The chasm disappears. Our estrangement is transformed into presence together. There may be tears, but behind them is joy.

Repentance may occur even in the life of a nation. It is a point of new beginning when a leader of a nation, no longer covering up the past, can say, "We were wrong. We made mistakes." As he speaks for us all, it becomes a time of national cleansing. In the power of faith such words can be spoken, transformation occur, and our estrangement from one another in the nation grow toward restored community.

When the past is changed by forgiveness, repentance becomes possible, and the present as well as the past is renewed. We are freed again to love and to act anew. We are freed from the blindness in which we stumbled along, not knowing what we were doing. The Cross transforms our vision so that we can see, not with complete clarity, but at least in a mirror dimly. H. Richard Niebuhr writes:

> We can discern in the contemporary confusion of our lives the evidence of a pattern in which, by great travail, . . . a work of redemption goes on which is like the work of Christ. We learn to know what we are doing and what is being done to us—how by an infinite suffering of the eternal victim we are condemned and forgiven at the same time; how an infinite loyalty refuses to abandon us either to evil or to nothingness. . . . The story of Jesus, and particularly of his passion, is the great illustration

that enables us to say, "What we are now doing and suffering is like this." (16.125)

When the past and present are transformed, the future comes alive with new possibilities that we were unable to see before. We must struggle still, but now there is hope. The seeming contradiction, Frederick Buechner reminds us, "is resolved when you realize that for Jesus peace seems to have meant not the absence of struggle but the presence of love" (6.69).

When we know ourselves forgiven, we are enabled to forgive others. Even more, when we dwell in our faith that God has forgiven our enemy, we are already on the way to being able ourselves to forgive that person. Thus the Cross transforms the estrangement of sin and guilt into the forgiving presence of God in our midst, drawing together and reshaping our common life. This heritage of our faith is proclaimed in Ephesians:

> Remember, you were once apart from Christ, aliens to the community of Israel, estranged from the covenant promises, in a world without hope and without God. The difference now is that in Christ Jesus you have been brought near through his blood. Jesus is our peace, healing the divisions among us and reconciling us to God in one community by means of the Cross. (Eph. 2:12-16)

When we stand at the Cross, there is no distinction among us—no Jew, no Gentile, no insider, no outsider, no stranger, no alien. The word of forgiveness is for us all. When we hear that word and receive it, we who were estranged are welcomed home into the presence and love of God.

A Prayer

God of history, Creator of our lives, we pray that the Cross of Christ may bring to us new perspectives and perceptions. Open our eyes that we may see Calvary both as mirror reflecting our image as we are, not knowing what we are doing, and as power disclosing the faithful action by which we are transformed.

Forgive our acts of ignorance or foolishness or selfishness whereby we have gone astray. Forgive our betrayals, our rejections, our acts of evil, whereby we have inflicted pain and suffering. We have cried for salvation in the wilderness of our inner frustrations and turmoil but often have not seen the new visions when they appeared. We have sought the secret of abundant and eternal life but have feared to let go of the narrow confines of familiar miseries and disappointments. Free us, we pray, from the sin and guilt that weigh us down and make us feel distant from your presence.

We thank you for the storytellers who have carried forward the record of faith—prophets who imaged the future, psalmists who voiced our inner longing, evangelists who preserved precious events and conversations, and Jesus, who used parable to convey what it means to be true and who embodied your faithfulness to us in his life and death.

Bless in us the powers of observation by which we gain awareness and empathy, the ability to imagine how we can change, the sensibility that makes us more human, more loving.

We pray in the name of Jesus Christ, who was faithful unto death, whose words of forgiveness are our assurance of your transforming presence among us. Amen.

2. Redemption:
Helplessness Transformed into Hope

"Truly, I say to you, today you will be with me in Paradise."
—Luke 23:43 RSV

Three execution trees, with their victims, have been thumped into place on Golgotha, and the scene around them is one of chaos. As Jesus hangs suffering and helpless on his cross, the soldiers gamble for the very clothes off his back and offer him bitter wine to suck from a sponge. People crowd around for a better look at this unfortunate criminal, labeled a joke before the world as "the King of the Jews." The taunts reach his ears: "You who would destroy the temple and build it in three days, save yourself! If you are the Son of God, come down from the cross" (Matt. 27:40 RSV).

Most vocal of the insulters and mockers, we are told, are the chief priest and the scribes and elders. At last they have Jesus where they want him, impotent and powerless. "He saved others," they cry with derision, "he cannot save himself. He is the King of Israel; let him come down from the cross, and we will believe in him. He trusts in God; let God deliver him now . . . ; for he said, 'I am the Son of God'" (Matt. 27:42-43 RSV).

And there are also the two criminals who hang crucified on either side of Jesus. Matthew and Mark tell us that both of these men, writhing in the same pain, revile Jesus, taunting him for his helplessness. "Are you not the Christ? Then save yourself and us!" they yell at him. But Luke records a different story. He writes that one of the criminals did not abuse Jesus, nor did he let the derision of the other go unchallenged. He turned and rebuked his companion with these words: "Do you not fear God, since you are under the same sentence of condemnation? And we indeed justly; for we are receiving the due reward of our deeds; but this man has done nothing wrong." Then he turned to Jesus and said, "Remember me when you come into your kingdom." To which our Lord replied, "Truly, I say to you, today you will be with me in Paradise" (Luke 23:40*b*-43).

This second word of Christ from the cross is a word of redemption. Jesus does not judge or condemn this guilty party. He doesn't say, "It's a little late for you to repent" or "Don't bother me now, I have enough trouble of my own" or any of the responses we might have made. Jesus' voice comes like a breath of fresh air, and his words bring new life to a dying thief. The criminal who has done wrong and is paying the penalty has at last done something right. In sheer desperation he has blurted out a crazy request to as unlikely a person as he might ever encounter, a person as seemingly powerless as himself. Lo, and behold, his request is heard; his life is changed; his helplessness is transformed into hope.

Indeed, Jesus said from the beginning that his ministry was for people such as this one being executed beside him. Those now present who had heard Jesus read from the book of Isaiah in the synagogue three years before may have felt the impact of that passage from the prophet echoing on Calvary:

> The Spirit of the Lord is upon me,
> because God has anointed me to preach good news to the poor.
> God has sent me to proclaim release to the captives

> and recovering of sight to the blind,
> to set at liberty those who are oppressed,
> to proclaim the acceptable year of the Lord.
>
> (Luke 4:18-19 RSV)

The scripture is fulfilled yet anew on this day Jesus is crucified.

The thief on the cross beside Jesus discovered what the crowd with its mocking words, the chief priests and scribes with their self-righteous taunts, the other criminal with his bravado, could not perceive. It was not Christ on the cross who was helpless, but rather those around him. God was in Christ even there on Calvary; what seemed to be weakness was the loving presence that redeems and transforms. Jesus' words expressed the faithful action of God that was embodied in Jesus' life. As John Baillie tells us in *Invitation to Pilgrimage:*

> Christ did not come to earth to tell us merely what we ought to do; He came to do something for us. He came not merely to exhort but to help. He did not come to give us good advice. That, if it were no more than that, was possibly not a thing of which we stood greatly in need, for there are always plenty of people who are ready with their advice. Advice is cheap, but what Christ offered us was infinitely costly. It was the power of God unto salvation. (2.51)

Jesus did not counsel the thief on how to atone for his past mistakes; Jesus gave himself to this fellow sufferer—forever.

In the light of this kind of strength it is we, we who take our places around the cross, who are revealed to be the helpless ones—not Jesus. The chief priests were helplessly in the grip of their lust for personal power; they could do nothing else but lash out at this good man who threatened them. Pilate found himself helpless before the danger of being denounced as "no friend of Caesar," so he set Barabbas free and let Jesus be crucified. The centurions were helplessly "doing their job," performing their cruelties as have millions of people before and since who acted only in obedience to orders. The crowd— Kierkegaard's "crowd" of irresponsibility—was a helpless mob, driven by mass anger and morbid curiosity, ill-informed, misdirected, blinded by its own emotional energy. The criminals were helpless, enmeshed in their own crimes, apprehended and condemned.

The cross on Calvary reveals the truth about our human existence. We are the helpless ones. Dorothy Sayers, in her play-cycle *The Man Born to Be King,* reminds us of this condition through words spoken by the women of Jerusalem:

> Alas! alas! . . . Poor man! . . . He preached so beautifully. . . . He spoke so sweetly. . . . He healed the sick. . . . He fed the hungry. . . . He was always so kind to children. . . . How sad, how sad to die so young! . . . Barely thirty years old, and handsome as young King David! . . . Cut off in the flower his strength. . . . Oh, dear! oh, dear! how sad it all is—I can't help crying. . . . Jesus! Jesus of Nazareth! We're all so sorry! . . . Speak to us! . . . Let us hear your voice again. . . . Comfort us, comfort us, son of consolation! . . .

To which Jesus replies:

> Daughters of Jerusalem, shed no tears for me. Weep for yourselves and for your children. For the time is coming when they will say, "Happy is the woman that never bore a child, and the empty arms that have no one to love or

care for." And they will flee to the hills; and creep into the earth for hiding, and cry to the mountains: "Fall down on us! fall, and cover our misery!" (21.294)

We are not called to Calvary to weep for Jesus. We are the helpless ones. When we truly dwell in the drama of the crucifixion, brought face to face with the suffering Christ, we know this reality beyond the shadow of a doubt.

There at the Cross of Jesus, however, we also discover something else. We are helpless, but we are not hopeless. Jesus speaks to us the same word of redemption he spoke to the condemned criminal beside him, transforming our helplessness into hope: "Today you will be with me in Paradise." What his crucified companion discovered that day on Golgotha the Christian church later proclaimed as its central belief. Paul speaks for us when he says:

> At the time when we were still helpless, Christ died for us who were without God. A person is unlikely to die willingly even for someone who is good, though a few might risk death for a really righteousness person. Yet God discloses the divine love for us in that Christ dies for us while we are helplessly enmeshed in sin. . . . If as enemies we are reconciled to God through the death of Jesus, we can be even more sure that we are saved by Jesus' life now that we have been reconciled. And so we are joyous in God through our Lord Jesus Christ, who has brought reconciliation to us. (Rom. 5: 6-8, 10-11)

We who are helpless sinners are redeemed by the Cross of Christ and given the promise of eternal presence with him. Our lives are transformed, our future is filled with hope, we are empowered to live forward in anticipation of God's abiding love.

All this we discover, not from the priests or the officials or the leaders or the law-abiding populace, but from the thief. It is this condemned criminal who does the one thing all of us must do if we are to know the transforming power of God's presence. He entreats Jesus, "Remember me when you come into your kingdom. Let it not be that my name and everything I am is blotted out. In spite of what I have done I yearn to count for something." Here there is no arrogant plea as was presented by the disciples James and John when they asked to sit on each side of Jesus in his kingdom. Here is a deep cry from the depths of a helpless, dying soul who asks simply to be remembered.

Those who set great store in confessions and statements of belief and doctrinal formulations for repentance may have trouble when they dwell in this exchange on Calvary. There is no indication that the thief believed in Jesus as his Savior or as the Son of God, but for Jesus the longing for presence with him is enough. There is no evidence the thief had great remorse for his past life of crime—he accepted his verdict of guilty without protesting the death sentence it carried. This hardly seems the proper attitude for repentance. Yet hanging there on the cross next to Jesus something came over him that partakes of the nature of repentance. Frederick Buechner sheds new light on this old familiar word when he suggests: "To repent is to come to your senses. It is not so much something you do as something that happens. True repentance spends less time looking at the past and saying, 'I'm sorry,' than to the future and saying 'Wow!' " (6.79). We don't know what the crucified thief said after Jesus answered his request, but it may well have been the Aramaic equivalent of "Wow!"

The priests, the officials, the soldiers, the milling crowd of onlookers, all yearn to feel powerful and in control. They try to overcome their nagging suspicions that they are not as good or holy as they profess to be, by destroying the one who makes them feel uncomfortable. Unlike them, the thief has no position to retain, no good name to protect, no authority to placate, no neck to save. He knows he is not good and turns to one beside him whose courage in the face of the derision and hostility has awakened his admiration. "Jesus, remember me." More than anyone else on Calvary the thief knows he is helpless and turns to Jesus in the hope that he will not be forgotten.

Having nothing to lose, this unnamed companion on the cross takes a chance on Jesus—and is given riches beyond his wildest dreams. Rather than granting the request and saying, "Sure, I'll remember you when I come into my kingdom," Jesus expresses the new and unimaginable promise "Today you will be with me in Paradise." There will be no waiting—beyond the agony of the next few hours anyway—it's going to be *today!* And it's not going to be an occasional, nostalgic memory either, for *you will be with me!* And it's not going to be when I reign with some kind of kingly power in this world. We'll be together in *Paradise*—you will be with me in the eternal covenant of God's love.

No one is placed on hold or made to wait outside while God conducts more important business. Even as the father in Jesus' parable of the prodigal son went eagerly to meet his child who was returning home, so God sees our repentance coming while we are still far away and hurries to meet us. Our very repentance is also our reconciliation. If we cannot say to God, "I'm sorry," if we are too lost in our guilt or our confusion or our despair to say to Jesus, "Forgive me," it will be enough to blurt out, "Remember me when you are engaged in your work of creation!" In saying those words with our whole hearts, our eyes may be opened to see that we already are part of the loving, redeeming activity of God.

The story of the Cross calls us to become like the thief, aware of our helplessness and our need to be remembered. Herein is our possibility for redemption and reconciliation, for here we are finally open to the transforming love of God. The thief experienced what Howard Thurman describes when he writes:

> The sins, bitterness, weakness, virtues, loves, and strengths are all gathered and transmuted by His love and His grace, and we become whole in His Presence. This is the miracle of religious experience—the sense of being totally dealt with, completely understood, and utterly cared for. (24.122)

Into his suffering and agony comes a sense of wholeness. All is not lost. I am accepted where I am. I am cared for. I am loved. And this gift is given to me not as a reward for something I did or as payment for work accomplished, it is given to me because in desperation I asked a dying companion to remember me. Can it really be true?

Why not? Things indeed are not what they seem. Those who appeared strong were weak and helpless. He who appeared weak and helpless was strong. The dying embers of hope are rekindled in the heart, and the new flame is the transforming power of our redemption.

A Prayer

God of the lost sheep and the safe flock, be to us the good shepherd who cares for us and remembers us this day.

It is hard for us to admit that we are often helpless. Save us from our fear of weakness and death by which we cling to false securities and decaying semblances of life. Rebuke the mocker and the scoffer that lurks beneath our superficial acceptance of those who seem more powerless than we. By the agony of your suffering on Calvary, may we be shocked and sickened into seeing our own insensitivity, self-righteousness, and exclusiveness.

Help us to be open to the possibility of your acceptance of us where we are, your presence with us as we are, that we may be redeemed from our helplessness and know again the transforming power of hope. Help us to do the one thing we can't seem to do by ourselves—help us to ask you for help. Enable us to go into our despairs, ambiguities, questions, longings; for there is where we will find the aching places that need your healing touch. Enable us to go into our loves, passions, joys, pleasures; for there we need your focus and blessing.

Keep us honest, O God, with ourselves, with others, and with you. Forbid that we should act according to some stereotyped notion of how a person of faith should act. If we can perceive any truth this day, may it be that the thief asked to be remembered out of his true need and Jesus gathered him into your loving covenant. Come to us in all the secret places of our hearts, and save us from ourselves that we might become ourselves in you. And may we always eat and drink in the remembrance that Christ died for sinners like us. Amen.

3. Comfort:
Pain Transformed into Action

"Woman, behold your son! . . .
Behold your mother!"

—*John 19:26, 27 RSV*

The suffering of Jesus on Calvary grows deeper and more intense. His sphere of awareness grows narrower and more personal. The derisive insults have died down. Some soldiers continue their gambling while others find various ways to pass the time until their three charges finally die. People who came out of curiosity to see the crucifixion of this "King of the Jews" are drifting away. Onlookers who taunted Jesus to use his reputed miraculous powers to save himself, half hoping he'd do it and show up the authorities, half fearing he might come down from the cross and tear into them, have given up in disappointment and relief. It has been an execution like any other as far as they can see, except perhaps for a strange feeling whenever they really look at the one in the middle.

Jesus has spoken only twice during the early frenzy that swirled around him—both were responses to actions outside himself. When the soldiers nailed him to his cross and dropped it into the ground, he asked God to forgive them because they didn't know what they were doing. Then as the mockery reached its peak and the criminal next to him asked to be remembered, Jesus told him they would be together in Paradise that very day.

Now as the crowd drifts away, certain individuals around the cross take distinct shape. From under his sweaty, bloodstreaked eyelids, Jesus recognizes faces and forms of people familiar and dear to him. Nearby stands Mary Magdalene, and beside her is Mary the mother of James the Younger and Joses, and Salome. All around him he sees the many women who came with him from Galilee—women not like those of Jerusalem who wept over him with such pity while begging for his words of comfort, but women who had cared for him and ministered to him with all they had to give. There at the edge of the group is the rich Joseph of Arimathea, a recent follower. Here close to the cross is the mother of James and John, those sons of Zebedee who were disciples from the beginning. Once, Jesus remembers, their mother urged him to promise that her two sons could sit on either side of him in his kingdom. And, yes, there with her is one of those sons, the beloved disciple John, the only one of the Twelve Jesus can see on Calvary.

And there is his own mother.

How Jesus' heart must have cracked anew, a heart already wrenched with physical pain and disappointment at this end to his ministry. His mother, always so proud of him, so concerned for his safety, so fearful of the threats to him, so lovingly devoted to trying to care for him, what will happen to her now? What can he possibly say to her to ease her suffering? She had never really understood what it was he was about, that he must give himself to the whole world, that all people were his family—his mother, father, sister, brother. How can he enable her to bear this terrible, tortured time?

Nowhere does the humanity of Jesus and his suffering strike closer to our own experience than as his mother stands beside the cross, broken and mourning. Any parents who have tended a child, loved that growing body, hoped for a long and happy life for this flesh of their flesh, can imagine what it would be like to stand in Mary's place. Whose heart would not break to see a beloved son die the death of a common criminal? Who of us has not watched one we love suffer, and felt the pain as our own, burning in us worse perhaps because we could do nothing to help? Not only is there the terrible pain of nails tearing into flesh, there is this additional suffering—Mary's, because she must watch her son suffer what she cannot share, and Jesus', because he knows what his mother is feeling.

What Jesus does is what he has done over and over before when words were not enough—he performs an act. His word of comfort is the outward expression of an inner relationship of loving faithfulness. By speaking, he summons the mourners to lay hold of the supportive interaction possible in their midst. John's own account of the exchange is powerfully simple: "When Jesus saw his mother, and the disciple whom he loved standing near, he said to his mother, 'Woman, behold your son!' Then he said to the disciple, 'Behold your mother!' And from that hour the disciple took her to his own home" (John 19:26-27 RSV).

Jesus comforts his mother by giving her the ongoing presence of one who will care for her as a son—not a man of great wealth or security, but a follower who shared the life and vision of Jesus' ministry. Mary will be able to talk of her son with someone who knew and loved him too. What stories these two must have shared in those days and years that followed! "Remember the time at Cana when he changed the water into wine?" "Or when he raised Lazarus?" "Remember when he fed the huge crowd, walked on the sea, healed the blind man?"

"Remember how he called himself the Good Shepherd and how he said he and God were one and that he had to die in order to be with us?" "Remember when he said the important thing is to love one another as he loved us?" Those long reminiscences must have comforted Mary through many a lonely hour, evoking Jesus through the power of memory, making him present again.

Jesus comforts John too. Helplessly watching his teacher die in torment, John is jarred into activity by Jesus' words. Caring for the mother of his Lord is a sacred and important task, a new focus for his love and commitment. John and his brother, James, known as "the sons of thunder" during those three years with Jesus, were subject to moods. Their enthusiasm could become depression all too easily. Now John won't be able to sink into despair and self-pity. He will be too busy making arrangements, seeing that Mary is made comfortable, looking after her needs. Perhaps as John and Mary talked through their grief with each other they filled the disciple's storehouse of memory with what would one day become a Gospel record of Jesus. John's pain was transformed by Jesus into action, enabling him to tell the story of his Savior to a world in need. And this story continues to empower new experiences and new actions through time.

Brother James was killed by Herod shortly after the Christian church got underway, the first of the Twelve to be martyred for his faith (Acts 12:2). Tradition tells us, however, that John lived to be a very old man; the Son of Thunder became the Beloved Disciple, testimony to the power of the transforming Cross.

And Jesus comforts himself. He can rest in the

assurance that these two persons so dear to him will be taken care of after he is gone. Unable to reach out to touch with tenderness the face of his mother, to grasp with courage the arm of John, Jesus still gives them himself by giving them each other. What Jesus does not say to his mother is as revealing perhaps as what he does say. He does not tell her to go home, that she shouldn't have come. He does not say: "Don't cry, it will be all right" or "I'm sorry I've brought you suffering" or "I can't stand to have you see me this way." Any of those expressions would only increase the agony and sorrow rather than bring comfort. Jesus knew the power of human emotions, and he knew the need for human presence together in times of anguish.

In an interview for the British Broadcasting Company, a woman who was dying of cancer made an astonishing observation about Jesus and his mother at the cross. The interviewer, a member of the clergy, confessed that when his turn came to die he would like to go away to some secret place where people would look after him so his wife and children would be spared the heartache of seeing him "go a bit peculiar in the head or go in a coma, and all this sort of stuff." The woman, from the depth of her pain and sense of her imminent death, sustained in her task of dying by her faith, made this reply:

> Our Lord carried his cross to Calvary and his mother followed him. And she was the sort of mother who would stand at the foot of the cross when her son was crucified. And he was the sort of son who would let her. And what more perfect love, and what more perfect understanding could there be than that. And can't you let us do the same? Can't we love each other in that way—in him? (8.0)

This woman illumines both the human condition in general and Jesus' word of comfort to his mother in particular. Jesus does not turn his mother away, even though her staying means she sees the horror of his death. He knows that for her to be prevented from keeping her vigil would be worse than the sorrow she feels in being present. He gives comfort to her through words that break down the isolation of her personal grief.

Jesus' sense that comfort comes as our pain is transformed into action is borne out in our own life experience. All of us have known sorrow in many forms. It comes as loneliness when a loved one is gone, as remorse and guilt that we did not do more for people while they were with us. Sorrow is the bitterness we feel at failing to attain our intended purposes; it is the pounding with our fists against the blank walls that human limitation forces us to accept. In our pain and sorrow, we feel a pent-up force that presses inside us, an accumulation of emotional energy like both a wildness and a despair. When we are able to "do something," we release the pressure and start on our way to healing. A friend is ill, and we cook food to take to the house. We worry over another and find ourselves pacing the floor, knitting furiously, cleaning the house, doodling, crying. When a loved one dies, we throw ourselves into the tasks that need to be done—planning the service, making the arrangements, meeting relatives as they arrive. And when the funeral is over, we gather to eat and talk. Pain is transformed into action.

We have mourned much in our time—not only personally but communally. War upon war has left few homes untouched. Death in auto collisions is the black plague of our day. Those unscathed by war or accident often seem to be at the mercy of an evil world that draws them into greed, drugs, crime, aimless drifting. We may laugh and make excuses, but it does not hide our sorrow. We know the need for Isaiah's words of hope:

> Comfort, comfort my people, says your God.
> Speak tenderly to Jerusalem, and cry to her
> that her warfare is ended, that her iniquity is pardoned,
> that she has received from the Lord's hand
> double for all her sins.
>
> (Isa. 40:1-2 RSV)

The suffering that is at the heart of life is also at the heart of the Scriptures. Israel and Jesus are called to bear the pain of the world, and the mystery is that through their suffering we are given healing and new life, enabling us to share one another's burdens. So Paul assures the people of Corinth:

> Blest be the God of our Lord Jesus; the Creator of mercies and all comfort, who provides solace in our troubles and enables us to comfort, others in their affliction with that same solace God has given us. Just as we share richly in the suffering of Christ, so we partake also of God's comfort through Christ. (II Cor. 1:3-5)

"Blessed are all who mourn," Jesus said, "for they will find comfort" (Matt. 5:4). Here Jesus tells us it is not just all right to be sorrowful, it is good. And the reason it is good is that in order to receive comfort we must first be able to mourn. Those who do not allow themselves to be emotional, who always keep a stiff upper lip, who refuse to let any experience hurt them, will remain forever uncomforted and "uncomfort-able." Trying to keep pain out of our lives does not spare us grief, it merely prevents our release from that grief; for the pain comes quite apart from our ability to will it away.

Oftentimes, it is fear of pain that enslaves more completely than could any suffering. Alan Paton recognizes this condition in *Cry, the Beloved Country,* when Father Vincent trys to comfort Stephen Kumalo:

—My friend, your anxiety turned to fear, and your fear turned to sorrow. But sorrow is better than fear. For fear impoverishes always, while sorrow may enrich.

Kumalo looked at him, with an intensity of gaze that was strange in so humble a man, and hard to encounter.

—I do not know that I am enriched, he said.

—Sorrow is better than fear, said Father Vincent doggedly. Fear is a journey, a terrible journey, but sorrow is at least an arriving.

—And where have I arrived, asked Kumalo.

—When the storm threatens, a man is afraid for his house, said Father Vincent in that symbolic language that is like the Zulu tongue. But when the house is destroyed, there is something to do. About a storm he can do nothing, but he can rebuild a house. (17.106)

We can work for justice and abundant life, but when injustice and tragedy wreak their destruction, we can do nothing except endure them—suffer them. If beyond our fear and our bitterness and our guilt we are able truly to mourn, we will be able at last to find comfort, and discover the courage to struggle again against malevolent powers.

Jesus' word of comfort to his mother speaks to all of us who hurt. "Behold your son, your mother, your daughter, your father, your friend!" Let us look around, step outside the small world of our own suffering, and do something. By God's grace our pain can be transformed into some action that makes the pain bearable. In sharing the agony within and without us, we will find comfort and strength to live on, a wider love to empower our fainting spirits.

A Prayer

O God, friend of Abraham and Sarah, friend of Moses, of Ruth, of Isaiah, of Mary and John, friend of Jesus, friend of ours:

We are grateful that you have created us in your covenant of peace and that your steadfast love for us is stronger than our broken promises, our apathy and carelessness, our acts of destruction and inhumanity. We confess our need to have laid upon us again your word of comfort and healing. We stand immobilized before the pain of the world, fearful to move lest our own hearts break, eager to heal yet anxious not to have our own lives infected with misery.

Give us, we pray, a vision of peace and comfort for our day that will summon us to active wrestling with our problems in excitement and enthusiasm. Help us to find with Moses the peace and comfort of the burning bush whereby we are expowered to lead the captives out of bondage. Help us to realize with Isaiah and Ezekiel the peace and comfort of exile in which we know our true home and dwelling place to be in you. Enable us to rejoice in the task of peace and comfort with Paul, even when that task leads us to share in the suffering of the crucified Prince of Peace. The measure of our covenants can be seen in what we love and in what gives us pain. Help us to live with courage the commitments of our love to whatever consequence they bring us.

We would bring comfort to those who mourn, O God, opening ways for your transforming power to turn pain into acts of love for each other. Enable us to live the faith we can imagine in our minds and which we so earnestly long for in our hearts. We pray in the name of Jesus, who is our peace, our comfort, and our covenant. Amen.

4. Loneliness:
Despair Transformed into Faith

"My God, my God, why have you forsaken me?"
—*Mark 15:34*

The drama on Calvary continues to unfold. It becomes increasingly difficult to watch these three figures as they writhe on their crosses. The soldiers and others who keep the vigil grow more and more quiet. This is not an execution over in a few minutes—gas pellets released, a gallows trap sprung, a volley of shots fired. To die by crucifixion is hard work; it takes time, painful time. As the hours creep by, there is every opportunity for the victim to feel the pain as it moves from wounded hands and feet and head growing numb to the ache of weight pulling on arms and shoulders, to feel the agony of each desperate breath forced through constricted lungs pressed hard against the ribs.

It is now about noon, the sixth hour after sunrise. Yet the day is neither bright nor clear. A dimness hides the sun. For the next three hours as it grows even darker, Jesus' attention continues to turn inward. He has forgiven his tormentors and the thief; he has given up his mother and disciple—it is all he can do for others in this place with him. Jesus must attend to his own dying and death. He must cope with his pain-wracked body and desolate spirit. The external world recedes from consciousness until all that remains of reality is pain. In that small, confined world of tortured suffering, Jesus is alone.

From the depths of that lonely world of anguish Jesus speaks for the fourth time, and the words chill our bones: "My God, my God, why have you forsaken me?" We who are witnesses at Calvary would like it better if Jesus had never uttered that cry. A strong, courageous death is what we want to see—Socrates drinking the hemlock so calmly while conversing with companions, Nathan Hale uttering immortal words of patriotism before enemies of the Revolution hang him, Keats dying of tuberculosis at twenty-eight but assuring his friend it is all right. If they can do it, we can do it. Or better yet, since they die so well, maybe we won't have to do it at all.

Indeed, Jesus' words trouble our minds as they break our hearts. Their expression of despair uncovers our own despair beneath our bravado; their echo of isolation and loneliness evokes in us our own haunting sense of aloneness. If Jesus, the incarnation of God, the Messiah, the Savior of the world, feels forsaken, what hope is there for us poor and utterly human creatures? Viewed from the standpoint of human reason there are no more embarrassing words in the Gospels than this cry of anguish wrung from Jesus on the cross. His pitiful plea seems to make nonsense of our carefully constructed Christologies. It appears to contradict our faith that God was in Christ.

Even those standing at the cross do not want to believe

their ears. They do not have to strain to hear these words of Jesus because he cries them with a loud voice. Still, Jesus says, "Eloi, Eloi, lama Sabachthani?" which means "My God, my God, why have you forsaken me?" and the bystanders try to find another meaning, saying to each other, "Listen, he is calling Elijah." One person runs to fill a sponge full of vinegar, puts it on a reed, and gives it to Jesus to drink, suggesting, "Wait, let's see whether Elijah comes to take him down" (Mark 15:35-36). Those bystanders are determined to have a sensational miracle. "Don't just die on us; take some of this vinegar and pull yourself together. Try harder; maybe Elijah will come yet." If Elijah will only appear and save Jesus, *then* we can believe, *then* we won't have to feel guilty about this crucifixion, *then* we won't have to die ourselves—lonely and despairing.

But Jesus goes all the way down to the lowest depths of human suffering. Already he has experienced the loneliness of human abandonment during the long night before his crucifixion. In the Garden of Gethsemane he invited his disciples to share his lonely vigil, his spirit's struggle with the death to come, his last few hours of freedom there in the darkness. They dropped off to sleep before even an hour had passed. After his arrest, Jesus experienced the despair of human forsakenness as those who were closest to him fled in terror, denying that they had ever known him.

Through those difficult times, however, Jesus still had a strong sense of God's presence and purpose in him. Now, dying on the cross, even that sustenance seems to leave him. Here Jesus experiences the abandonment of the One in whom he placed his trust; he feels forsaken by God.

Why it should be this way for Jesus we do not know. We do know we are in the middle of a great mystery. For as we dwell in the crucifixion and listen to these agonizing words of Jesus, our feelings are strangely stirred, and we are led to deep reflection. In astonishment we realize that no other statement of Jesus strikes closer to the predicament in which human beings find themselves today. We live in a God-forsaken world, light years of infinite nothingness. No other feeling seems more characteristic of persons today than loneliness, anxiety, and despair. We fear that we are abandoned. We are desperately afraid of being alone. So we seek ways to fill the void in our lives—music, noise, pleasure, possessions. We turn on the television and try to live vicariously through the people depicted there. We huddle together with others like ourselves, those we know talk the same language and share the same values, manner of dress, style of relationship. But, like the other-directed person David Riesman describes vividly in *The Lonely Crowd,* we are still lonely because we never really get close to ourselves or to other people.

It is not so much that we have ceased to believe in God as that our guilt and estrangement makes us prey to the anxiety that God has abandoned us. Indeed, in the light of the injustices of our world and the explosive forces that humans have unleashed, we are afraid that God has forsaken us and know in our hearts that there is no good reason the Creator should not leave us to our own ways of self-destruction. It does not feel as though we live in a "world come of age" but in a world frantically childish or adolescent. Faced with serious problems of survival—the energy crisis, the environmental crisis, the nuclear crisis—we long nostalgically for the good old days when someone else took care of the problems. Like children gone off in the woods to play, we suddenly realize that we are alone, a feeling Thomas Wolfe voices for us with great poignancy:

> Naked and alone we came into exile. In her dark womb we did not know our mother's face; from the prison of her flesh have we come into the unspeakable and incommunicable prison of this earth.
>
> Which of us has known his brother? Which of us has looked into his father's heart? Which of us has not remained forever prison-pent? Which of us is not forever a stranger and alone?
>
> O waste of loss, in the hot mazes, lost, among bright stars on this most weary unbright cinder, lost! Remembering speechlessly we seek the great forgotten language, the lost lane-end into heaven, a stone, a leaf, an unfound door. Where? When?
>
> O lost, and by the wind grieved, ghost, come back again. (29.1)

Here we are in our loneliness. Here are the spikes driven into humanity's hands and feet, nailing us to our fear and anxiety.

But it is to this extremity of human beings at the limits of the world that the Cross speaks. Our God-forsaken despair is mirrored there. The chasm of estrangement between God and humankind finds flesh and blood. Jesus speaks for us on Calvary. His lonely words asking why God has forsaken him are not spoken for the martyrs, the saints, or those who are secure in their faith. Jesus speaks for us who feel lost and alone. In the words of Jügen Moltmann: "The God-abandoned Son of God takes the eternal death of the abandoned and the damned upon himself in order to become God of the abandoned and brother of the damned. Every person damned and abandoned by God can, in the crucified one, experience community with God" (13.15). Because Jesus on the cross experiences the worst that life has to offer, we know that he understands and is with us in all our times of suffering, loneliness, and despair. From the beginning of his ministry Jesus told his listeners that "it is not the healthy but rather the sick who need a physician. Go and learn the meaning of this: 'I desire mercy, not sacrifice.' Therefore, I do not call the righteous but sinners to repentance" (Matt. 9:12-13). When we feel cut off from God for whatever reason—physical pain, destructive pride, estrangement from others—behold, God is with us, sharing our suffering and calling us to new life.

When we feel farthest from God, we are perhaps closest to God. In our sense of being forsaken there is no longer any pretense, no rational cover-up of superficial credos that really come between us and the Creator. When we know we are alone, there is only raw human need, our own and that of others, that partakes of the suffering heart of God. Calvary becomes our assurance that human despair can be transformed into faith.

As Jesus speaks for us, voicing our own sense of lostness and despair, he also enables us to speak out ourselves, into and across whatever abyss exists between us and God. His petition is not a cry to some abstract void, but is the desperate prayer of one who has known and lost the sense of God's presence. Even in his feeling of abandonment Jesus addresses the God who seems absent; his despair, directed to the God in whom he believes, echoes the ancient Hebrew cry of prayer and praise:

My God, my God, why have you forsaken me?
Why are you so far from aiding me, in the midst of
my suffering?

(Ps. 22:1)

Jesus' word of loneliness bridges the distance and the
silence, giving voice to human feelings of isolation and
transforming despair into faith. The despair is real, but
underneath it God is there already. The cry is needed both
to relieve the pressure of pain and loneliness and to recall
God's continuing presence to the faltering spirit.

In many of his parables Jesus exhorted his followers to
seek God even when their efforts seemed useless: the
widow importuning the judge until he heard her case, the
person hammering on the neighbor's door until it opened.
Eventually our need will be met if we keep trying. By
acknowledging our despair, as Jesus did from the cross,
we may touch springs of faith in God hidden behind the
despair, allowing the healing waters to well up again.

Beyond the call to take our whole selves, our doubts,
our loneliness, our despair, to God, Jesus' cry of
abandonment by God reveals God to us and with us. For
on the cross there is not only full humanity, there also is
God. Paul's words come to us with new intensity: "God
was in Christ, reconciling the creation to the Creator" (II
Cor. 5:19*a*). Not only is God present to the suffering
Jesus, God is suffering in Jesus; becoming human, God
experiences the loneliness and the despair to which
human beings are subject.

In Jesus Christ, God suffers the pain of our rebellion
and loneliness. God is here crying in a loud voice to human
beings, "My people, my creatures, why have you forsaken

me?" Here is God reaching out to the farthest horizons of human desperation and reconciling it all within the covenant of love. God comes to us and shares our uncertainty, our tragedy, our forsakenness. We discover that the emptiness of our lives is but the reflected image of our faithlessness, an emptiness that becomes in the Cross the fullness of God's love. Charles Allen Dinsmore has put it most clearly and simply: "There was a cross in the heart of God before there was one planted on the green hill outside of Jerusalem" (7.7).

In this knowledge we see the suffering of God wherever there is human suffering. Elie Wiesel's book *Night* is the horrifying account of his own experiences as a boy of fifteen in a concentration camp. The author describes seeing two men and a young boy with "the face of a sad angel" hanged in the center of the camp. One man in the crowd of forced spectators kept asking, "Where is God?" The two men died immediately, but the light weight of the boy denied him a quick end.

> For more than half an hour he stayed there, struggling between life and death, dying in slow agony under our eyes, . . .
> Behind me, I heard the same man asking:
> "Where is God now?"
> And I heard a voice within me answer him:
> "Where is He? Here He is—He is hanging here on this gallows. . . ." (26.76)

God is crucified in Jesus, and God is crucified over and over—in the senseless slaughter of Jews in the Holocaust, in the deprivation of human rights around the globe, in child abuse, in the violation of nature. Wherever humans

65

suffer at the hands of hate and ignorance and evil, wherever humans hunger for dignity or food, God is crucified anew.

When we read the Bible, let us remember to do more than seek for answers it can give us; for the greatness of Scripture does not rest in its ability to solve problems. Let us enter the world of the Bible by listening first to the profound and penetrating questions it asks: "Am I my brother's keeper?" "Who is my neighbor?" "What is truth?" "What shall I do to inherit eternal life?"

Jesus' fourth word from the cross takes its place as one of those great and provocative questions of the Bible, "My God, my God, why have you forsaken me?" Those of us who find that this question is our question are not likely to discover a simple answer that satisfies human reason or philosophical speculation. But if we dwell in the question, we will be led to relate to others who ask the question. And by sharing the loneliness and abandonment together, we may find there the answer of the Cross—that God is with us in the Crucified One, whose own lonely suffering transforms our despair into faith.

A Prayer

O God of our journeys through the darkness and the light, God of our leave-taking and our home-coming and all our wandering in between, be with us now in this particular time and place.

Free us, we pray, from the personal demons in us that blind us to your healing presence as we journey in life. Help us to be able to be alone without being lonely, to be concerned without being anxious, to be miserable without being in despair. But if the darkness comes upon us and we are lost in the fear that we are abandoned and forsaken, then, O God, find some way to remind us of your own love in the crucified Jesus, sharing with us the worst that can happen to us and making it a channel of blessing and grace.

Give us courage to face our many fears. Help us to call out for help in times of storm and stress, that we, like the frightened disciples, may find the blessing of peace. Help us in our suffering to take the risk of touching the hem of Jesus' robe, that we, like the afflicted woman, may know the grace of healing. Help us to roll away the stone from the face of death itself, that we, like Jairus' daughter, like Lazarus, like Jesus, may be raised to new life.

By faith we pray we may be enabled to praise all things, believing that the light shines in the dark and the dark does not overcome it, that joy endures beyond pain and sadness, that love abides beyond death, that the new can come from the death of the old. Be to us a transforming power through whom our despair is turned to this faith and our lonely flesh is welcomed home to your creation. We pray in the name of the Crucified One who shares our humanity. Amen.

5. Suffering:
Need Transformed into Love

"I thirst."

—John 19:28 RSV

Time moves on slowly, relentlessly, at Golgotha. Surely the suffering and dying of those on the crosses cannot last much longer. But having passed the last three hours in spiritual anguish, crying at last to God his despair at being forsaken, Jesus now seems to rally. He lifts his head as one awakening from tortured dreams, conscious again of where he is, aware of the terrible pain that sheathes his body, but no longer lost in the lonely labyrinths of forsakenness.

We do not know whether God answers Jesus' question—if perhaps a comforting presence came to his heart or a sound of assurance echoed in his memory, if a cool breeze touched his fevered, wet cheek or an unseen dove descended again in his mind's eye. But it seems that *something* happened to Jesus. He endured the worst, hit the bottom of the black pit into which his spirit tumbled. Now he starts a slow return to the world in which his life still struggles for breath.

The bystanders who had hoped for a miracle are no doubt disappointed. As they stand waiting for Elijah, Jesus speaks a fifth time—but his words do not describe a vision of the old prophet coming in a chariot of fire from heaven. Jesus simply states his own need: "I thirst."

Oh how those two words evoke in us a deep feeling of kinship to Jesus in his suffering. Our own remembrance of what it is like to be thirsty comes to us in a flash—not particular events, perhaps, which faded when the thirst was slaked, but certainly the memory of the feeling. We have only to dwell in that statement "I thirst" for a moment, and the longing for water comes vividly alive. We become conscious of the dry mouth and burning throat, the deep craving inside us that we know can only be soothed by a drink of water. How many times a day do we fill a glass with liquid and swallow it without thinking, taking it for granted? Perhaps we instinctively try to fill an internal store of water against the day when we must wait and endure the experience of being thirsty. When we need a drink, however, it doesn't matter how much or when we last had something.

Jesus has been hanging on the cross for some six hours in the heat of the late morning and early afternoon. The last he had to drink may well have been the wine he blessed and shared with his disciples in that upper room the previous evening—the wine that he told them was his "blood of the new covenant, poured out for many" (Mark 14:24). Breathing with great effort through open mouth, feverish as he struggles with the unremitting pain, Jesus acknowledges, so truly human, that he is thirsty.

Yet no one goes running for a cup of cool water. "A bowl of sour wine was nearby; so they soaked a sponge in the wine and on a hyssop stalk held it up to his mouth" (John 19:29). How could they do such a thing? Perhaps there was no water nearby, and this was the best to be offered. Perhaps the vinegary wine was provided as a means to dull his sense of pain, a kind of tranquilizer. Perhaps the same ones who tried to give the sour beverage when he cried in despair to God want to try again to get him to rouse Elijah. The reason at the moment is not clear, but later, as we reflect on the events at Calvary, we will remember Jesus' experience was like the psalmist's:

> Insults have broken my heart,
>   so that I am in despair.
> I looked for pity, but there was none;
>   and for comforters, but I found none.
> They gave me poison for food,
>   and for my thirst they gave me
>   vinegar to drink.

> (Ps. 69:20-21 RSV)

There seems to be no end to the suffering Jesus must endure, not unlike the suffering servant proclaimed in Isaiah.

Jesus' words suggest a particular kind of self-awareness. He does not cry out "Water" or "Drink" as though responding to some vague physical urge. Jesus is conscious of his own thirst, and suffers it as a deep personal need. This man, who once told the people, "I am the bread of life; the person who comes to me shall not hunger, and the one who believes in me shall never thirst (John 6:35 RSV), this man knows that he himself is thirsty now. Jesus is not simply in pain, he is suffering.

Once again we feel that Jesus is speaking for us, for all of us who seek desperately for a way to quench the many thirsts of our lives. Too often, however, we look in the wrong places. We pursue pleasure that gives immediate satisfaction, but alas, our capacity for physical gratification is limited—we can only drink so much before we become sick, or we find that after a time nothing satisfies our thirst, and we become cynical about life. In his *Letters to a Young Poet*, Rainer Maria Rilke praises physical pleasure as a sensual experience that enhances our knowing of the world. But, he says, "the bad thing is that most people misuse and squander this experience and apply it as a stimulant at the tired spots of their lives and as distraction instead of a rallying toward exalted moments" (20.36). In this sense, sensual experience is enjoying the taste of water when we are thirsty, not just drinking to fill ourselves up; the latter leaves us thirsty again in a short time.

Even more than pleasure, perhaps, we today seek security from ever having to feel thirsty at all. We strive for peace of mind to fill our thwarted aspirations. The arms race and détente speak not so much for our efforts at peace but for national security. Our attempts to work out social security and tax relief do not reflect the depth of our charity but our striving for personal well-being.

And over against this seeking stands the Cross. We strive to avoid suffering; we find God accepting it. Peter fleeing Rome to escape execution meets Christ going to be crucified again. So with us all.

As we listen to this word of Jesus, "I thirst," we may wonder what he saw in his imagination as he summoned up images to ease his need. Much of Jesus' ministry was related to water. Did he feel again somehow the water of his baptism as he stood with John in the Jordan River? Did he remember the waves crashing against the boat on the Sea of Galilee arousing fear in his disciples, or the waves under his feet as he walked on the sea evoking their astonishment? Did he think of the water he turned into wine at the wedding feast, the water of his tears as he wept for Lazarus and for Jerusalem, the water of his spittle as he made clay to put on the eyes of the blind man before sending him to wash in the pool of Siloam and receive his sight? Did he recall the feel of the water as he washed the disciples' feet the night before?

In all his ministrations with water Jesus sought to meet the human needs he saw and to fill those needs with love. Now he is thirsty, and his own need is also an act of love. Having no water to give, he suffers his thirst and becomes united in love with all who are in need. The Cross, with its expression of divine suffering, stands as a challenge to every evasion of responsibility, every failure to answer human need. The world groans under the yoke of injustice. There is a divine *and* a human thirst for righteousness in a dry and thirsty land. The Cross recalls to memory the prophetic tradition of judgment: "Woe to those who are at ease in Zion, who oppress the poor, who crush the needy. Let justice roll down like waters, and righteousness like an everflowing stream" (Amos 6:1*a*, 4:1*b*, 5:24 RSV). Our God is a passionate God who feels the thirst of people and calls us to minister to the needs of our fellow humans. Wherever these acts of love occur, God is there. When the disciples complained to Jesus that a nonfollower was healing in his name, Jesus spoke with considerable force: "Do not prevent him. . . . I tell you truly, if a person gives you a cup of water to drink because you bear the name of the Christ, that person will not be denied a reward" (Mark 9:39*a*, 41).

Over all our narrow, selfish motivations and our preoccupation with security, the Cross broods. For those of us who think that the greatest goal of human endeavor is to avoid suffering, the Cross starkly discloses that we seek too easy an escape from tragedy, from responsibility, from life, from taking risks that may bring suffering but that also bring love. We must not cling to our own needs and feed on the hurt they cause us, but rather set out to meet the challenges of service to others in need. By piteously hugging our suffering to ourselves we stand in the way of our own possibilities for love. As Elizabeth Berryhill expresses it in a poem:

Love, unrequited, is love unused;
Thus festers and corrupts,

Sounds a strident, sour note,
Burns ice-cold,
Raises its head to the sky, howls,
Turns 'round on itself and bites its own tail,
Then foams at the mouth, bares its teeth and snarls,
Lies down. . . . and whimpers.

Love, unused, is love unrequited.
It is a riddle but there is an answer to it:
Use it, you fool,
Any way you can.

"Riddle"

Our need for love can be transformed into love when we are willing to use it for others and not just let it nourish our own pain.

We *can* act with intention; we are free to accept the circumstances that our acts of freedom bring us. Suffering is also part of our freedom, but when we become aware that we suffer and why we suffer, it becomes not a tragedy to be endured but a possibility for love. "Blessed are those who hunger and thirst for righteousness," Jesus assured us, "for they shall be satisfied" (Matt. 5:6 RSV).

If we cease to care about the thirst of the world for righteousness, or even our own thirst, we are dead to life. We will not feel the painful need, but neither will we experience the wild ecstasy of joy and love. "The most tragic thing of all, in the long run," Rollo May writes, "is the ultimate attitude, 'It doesn't matter.' The ultimately tragic condition in a negative sense is the apathy, the adament, rigid 'cool,' which refuses to admit the genuinely tragic" (10.111). Only when we desire the transformation can the need within us become love.

The Cross speaks to us of human suffering on many levels. There we see the basic need for water to alleviate physical thirst. Since this relief is always temporary, our efforts must be continuous. But there in the Cross we also see the deeper thirst for a "love that will not let us go." One time as Jesus journeyed through Samaria he stopped at a well and asked a woman for a drink. When she expressed surprise that a Jew would ask a Samaritan for water, Jesus suggested she might ask him for a drink also. But, he said, "whoever drinks of the water that I shall give will never thirst again; the water that I shall give people will become to them a spring of water welling up to eternal life" (John 4:14 RSV). This Crucified One who himself thirsts on the cross is the one who knows how to give us the living water of God's own love, sustaining us through all our suffering.

Why is it that we find in the Christ who is hurting, the power that is healing? Again we are back at the mystery. Suffering is an intrinsic part of life. Only a God with wounds can grasp the attention of wounded human beings and hold it long enough to start them on the way toward healing.

Thornton Wilder has explored this transformation of need into love in one of his early three-minute plays. An afflicted man makes his way to a pool that, when the angel causes the water to be troubled, has the power to heal. As he stands among the others who also wait in the hope they will be made whole again, the angel comes to him and says, "Draw back, physician, this moment is not for you. . . . Healing is not for you." The man pleads to be cured, that he might do even more for others as a whole person. Standing a moment in silence, the angel then speaks:

Without your wound where would your power be? It is your very remorse that makes your low voice tremble into the hearts of men. The very angels themselves cannot persuade the wretched and blundering children on earth as can one human being broken on the wheels of living. In Love's service only the wounded soldiers can serve. Draw back.

As the physician steps aside, the angel touches the water and the crowd throws itself into the rippling pool. A man whose crippled hand has been restored emerges jubilantly, then stops as he sees the afflicted physician. Sorrow replaces the joy, and he speaks urgently:

> May you be the next, my brother. But come with me first, an hour only, to my home. My son is lost in dark thoughts. I—I do not understand him, and only you have ever lifted his moôd. Only an hour . . . my daughter since her child had died, sits in the shadow. She will not listen to us. (27.147-49)

The wounded Jesus has the power to heal us; his thirst is the living water that restores us to wholeness.

And we who stand under this Cross are summoned to become servants of God. Thomas à Kempis disturbs our thoughts as to what that summons means when he writes in *The Imitation of Christ,* "Many there be to share the joys and comforts of Jesus, but few there be to bear his cross" (bk. II, chap. 11). To hear Jesus say to us, "Pick up your cross and follow me" is to find in ourselves the thirsting that neither ease nor security nor pleasure nor anything in all creation can fulfill. This is the thirst that is satisfied only as we join the community of suffering where our need is transformed into loving service.

A Prayer

Our God, creator of the dance of life, giver of bread and wine and joy, redeemer of all that is lonely and fearful and tight, we thank you for this day and for your presence with us right now.

You alone know our many thirsts and the suffering they have caused us and others. You alone know the ways we have tried to avoid responsibility for your creation, to escape our part in the suffering of the world, to deny the dryness in our mouths and in our eyes and in our hearts. You alone know how we try to meet our own needs and the despair that rises in us as our thirst remains unquenched.

Bless all the wounded soldiers in Love's service who minister through their afflictions. May your living water be an everflowing stream in their spirits to ease their suffering.

And give us, we pray, a taste of your living water, that we may be sustained in our search for how to be faithful and loving. Open our minds, free our tongues, release our spirits, put your rainstorm in our hearts. May we see in all who are hungry and thirsty the image of the Crucified One who spoke their need in his. Help us to labor, that what we do may be valuable, that others might yet be glad that we have lived and worked.

Shake us, move us, prod us, O God, that we may be enabled to bring something new out of the parched life around us. May we be water-bearers for thee, faithful even in the face of our dark needs, to the end that we may be opened to the fierce and transforming power of your love. We pray in the name of Jesus the Christ, who endured human thirst that we might taste the water welling up to eternal life. Amen.

6. Fulfillment:
Failure Transformed into Wholeness

"It is finished."
— *John 19:30*

The light of the sun has faded, and the shadows of the crosses lengthen across Calvary. Jesus, dying and thirsty, knows the end is near. Possibility is narrowing; the doors are closing; the curtain is falling. The drama of the crucifixion that earlier enveloped the whole landscape around Jerusalem and the place of the Skull now focuses only on Jesus. There is no concern for the crowds and soldiers, the loud talk and the weeping, the needs and supplications. Jesus has said, "I thirst," and the sponge with the sour wine has been extended to him on a reed of hyssop.

After Jesus receives the wine, he speaks for a sixth time: "It is finished."

It is finished. What mixed feelings this word arouses in us. Are we to be glad or sad to hear what we know already in the pit of the stomach? Yes, happy are we that at last the agony and the pain will be gone, that the lungs will be freed from the labored, rasping breath. But heartbroken too that his too brief life is over, that his death should come like this. Glad, yes, that the humiliation is ended, our shame released, that this cross will now be removed from our sight. And sad and grieved that we shall never again hear his voice, feel his touch—never be able to seek his counsel, listen to one of his stories, learn of God from his own lips.

Do we murmur among ourselves at the foot of the cross,

agreeing and consoling? Do we protest in a loud voice, "Don't leave us; you can't die"? Do we cry? Do we run away? Do we throw ourselves about in desperation? Do we accept with relief or vow revenge? Or faint? Or go crazy? Do we give up and count it all as loss, or do we go on living?

We know death most often and intimately as a terrible thing. Not only this kind of death, the violent wrenching away of life in its prime. And not just accidental death, which snatches us away without plan or reason. Death, any kind of death, means the end of our hopes and dreams, the end of *us*—this face in the mirror, this foot wiggling in its shoe, this hand holding a pencil. In the presence of death we weep not only for the dead but for ourselves who will die. We may wistfully regret dying as the psalmist who wrote:

> For all our days pass away under thy wrath,
>   our years come to an end like a sigh.
>   (Ps. 90:9 RSV)

Or we may rage at death as the final absurdity with Shakespeare's Macbeth:

> Life's but a walking shadow, a poor player
> That struts and frets its hour upon the stage,
> And then is heard no more; it is a tale
> Told by an idiot, full of sound and fury,
> Signifying nothing.
>   (act 5, scene 5)

Either way death stands before us at the end of our personal life. In time we all must say, "It is finished."

So often we try to deceive ourselves about this sure fact of living. Few ordinary happenings in modern life are so carefully concealed as is death. The deceased are dressed in their best clothes, color put on their faces, and their bodies stretched out on satin cushions as if asleep. We do not approach the grave, in William Cullen Bryant's words from "Thanatopsis," "like the quarry slave at night scourged to his dungeon"; yet neither do we seem to be "sustained and soothed by an unfaltering trust." Instead we treat death like an unfortunate mistake, a social error, a rip in the garment of existence that we must overlook, ignore, and pretend is not really there.

So to our ears Christ's words are a death knell we thought we had silenced. They strike a chord in our hearts of suppressed, familiar fear. They sound like resignation to the end that awaits all of us.

But is this a word only of resignation? To be sure, Jesus knew his life was coming to an end. He, Jesus, the man, was finished. There would be no more days and nights, no more flesh to bear in joy or sorrow. Certainly Jesus was resigned to this fact; he would die as dead as any human being. Suppose, however, that we listen to Jesus' word without hearing it simply as an echo of our fear and anxiety. What if we could hear Jesus saying a new thing, as he did so often throughout his ministry? Then we just might find in Jesus' statement not only finality but also fulfillment. "It is finished"—it is completed, wound up; it has been accomplished, brought together, consummated. Jesus has already done what Paul will later experience and write to Timothy—"fought the good fight, finished the race, kept the faith" (II Tim. 4:6 RSV).

It would be easy to look at Jesus' life and death in the

world's terms and write it off as a failure. At the very beginning of his ministry, when he spoke in the synagogue, he so aroused the wrath of the congregation that they almost killed him. His family didn't understand him. He called twelve special disciples to follow him—one was his betrayer and the rest deserted when the going got rough. He exasperated the moralists by taking meals with tax collectors and sinners and frustrated the radicals by refusing to lead an uprising. His acts of healing often brought out the anger of the priests and Pharisees. He provoked both the political leaders and the church authorities. He announced the reign of God, yet people remained in the yoke of the Romans. He preached the abundant life but had no worldly goods, not even a place to be buried. He encouraged love and was crucified for it.

Yet what to the eyes of the world may look like failure is, in the Cross, transformed into wholeness. Calvary judges our every inclination to measure the meaning of a life as if we were adding up the score of a game. Life is lived in covenants made with the self, with others, and with God. There is a sense in which Jesus could neither fail nor be defeated because his commitment was not primarily to himself and his cause. His commitment was to being faithful to God. He did not deliberately choose to suffer, but he was faithful to a way that brought suffering, and he did not seek to escape the consequences of his own free acts.

So it is for all of us. If we are dedicated to ourselves and to the limited goals we can envision, then we may well despair at our lack of success. But if we give ourselves to the highest cause, seeking active engagement in the task of being faithful to God, then there can be no failure.

Those who labor for social justice and human rights encounter many setbacks, but they are not defeated. Their cause is that of creation, and when they suffer, the whole world groans in travail. God has set the desire for freedom and justice and righteousness in the human heart, and though we may lose many battles, we will never lose the war. Our struggles are fulfilled in every moment, our failures transformed into wholeness by the crucified God who suffers with us. In the knowledge of this divine power, the author of Hebrews summons us to participate in the struggle:

> Therefore, since we are surrounded by so great a cloud of witnesses, let us also lay aside every weight, and sin which clings so closely, and let us run with perseverance the race that is set before us, looking to Jesus the pioneer and perfecter of our faith, who for the joy that was set before him endured the cross, despising the shame, and is seated at the right hand of the throne of God. (Heb. 12:1-2 RSV)

In July, 1967, the great African ex-Zulu chief Albert Luthuli was killed by a freight train while on his way to his cottage. This diligent worker for human justice had been "banned" in South Africa since 1959 and restricted to the area near his home without trial or recourse to the courts. He was forbidden to attend public gatherings or to make speeches or publish statements; but in spite of this, his labors against apartheid won him the Nobel Peace Prize for 1960. Speaking at the funeral for his friend Chief Luthuli, Alan Paton said:

> There are some people who will think that his life was a failure. Some will think he went too far and some that he

did not go far enough. But that is not the real story of his life. The real story of his life is the story of his fortitude. If you win in life, you are a successful man. If you lose, you are an unsuccessful man. But if you go on whether you win or lose, then you have something more than success or failure. You keep your own soul. In one way Luthuli lost the world, but he kept his own soul.

Although he was silenced, history will make his voice speak again, that powerful brave voice that spoke for those who could not speak. (18.206-7)

Beyond our efforts for justice, which the powers of the world can thwart, God still fulfills our work. The person who lived and worked is finished, but the life and the work of that person go on.

"We have this treasure in earthen vessels," Paul wrote to the Corinthians, "to show that the transcendent power belongs to God and not to us. We are afflicted in every way, but not crushed; perplexed, but not driven to despair; persecuted, but not forsaken; struck down, but not destroyed; always carrying in the body the death of Jesus, so that the life of Jesus may also be manifested in our bodies" (II Cor. 4:7-10 RSV).

We know that people who are dying often see their lives pass before their eyes. Perhaps Jesus also saw in his mind's eye the brief span of his years as he hung there on his cross becoming increasingly lightheaded, eyes blurry with agony and sweat, body numb with pain and fatigue. We may wonder what pictures appeared in those flashbacks! Did he see Nazareth and his carpenter's shop? Did he see his long-dead father? Perhaps he remembered the good times—early days with the disciples as he explained to them their mission, the crowds that listened eagerly to him speak, gatherings when the food was stretched to feed everyone, finding just the right story to tell, seeing people change and come alive as did Mary Magdalene, Nicodemus, Zacchaeus.

Perhaps Jesus remembered the hard times—being tempted in the wilderness, the execution of his cousin John the Baptist by Herod, the weariness he often felt as the people pressed in upon him, the loneliness of his prayers in the Garden, the flogging, the humiliation. Did he think of the stories his mother told of his birth? Did the faces of those he had healed appear to him again—the lepers, the demoniacs, the paralytics, the epileptics, the blind? Did the cries of "Hosanna" as he rode into Jerusalem on the donkey ring again in his ears? Did he weep again at the people's lack of understanding?

Reliving these bits and pieces, Jesus may well have wondered at the puzzle of his life. Experiences that were so vibrant when they happened had begun to fade. Could the energizing power of those times persist in spite of their fragmented nature and the passing of the years? Well, now it was finished. There was meaning in the bits and pieces, and Jesus' remembrance of them must have brought him peace. Now he could let go.

Hundreds of years later another martyr for the faith pondered on the fragmentariness of life. Dietrich Bonhoeffer, writing from prison to his friend Eberhard Bethge, said:

> The important thing today is that we should be able to discern from the fragment of our life how the whole was arranged and planned, and what material it consists of. For really, there are some fragments that are only worth throwing into the dustbin . . . , and others whose

importance lasts for centuries, because their completion can only be a matter for God, and so they are fragments that must be fragments. (5.219)

What is finished for Bonhoeffer and for Jesus in their executions are the fragments of their lives. But the fragments are enough, for each reflects a bit of the pattern of the whole, a wholeness that is shaped and consummated in God. Jesus did not have to die on Calvary, but in every fragment of his life there was present the love that would be willing, if necessary, to be nailed to the cross. Bonhoeffer did not have to be hanged by the Nazis, but his life reveals a spirit of faithfulness that led him to endure even death as the cost of his discipleship.

Jesus did not seem to share our dread fear of dying, for he pointed to that fulfillment of life and work that can only come in death. "Truly, truly, I say to you," Jesus told his disciples, "unless a grain of wheat falls into the earth and dies, it remains alone; but if it dies, it bears much fruit" (John 12:24 RSV). His appointed ministry on earth is finished, but it is only because it is over that it can even be spoken of as fulfilled. As long as we are in the flesh, our lives are not complete; they are fragmentary. To be finished, then, is to enter that fulfillment that is only possible through death.

In the last stanza of a poem about a man who is dying, Helen Berryhill voices this same perception:

> There is nobility in this room,
> This room of the spirit
> Where the hero from struggles
> Lies down to his rest.

As the openings are closing,
The stone rolls into place
And entombment releases.

(4.42)

The suffering, the pain, the struggle, are finished. By death we are freed from the bondage of death.

We all come to our dying with the fragments of our lives—some seemingly worthless failures, some bearing the patterns of our commitments and covenants. But this is not the entire story, as Paul perceived: "Now we see only dim reflections, but then we shall see face to face. Now I understand only in bits and pieces; then I will know fully, even as all along I have been completely known" (I Cor. 13:12). In death we know, with Jesus, that our life and work are finished, but we know too that there our incompleteness is fulfilled and our failures are transformed into the wholeness of God.

A Prayer

God of time, God of the times and of the timely, God of timelessness, we lift our hearts to you in prayer and praise this day.

We thank you for life—for our lives and for the lives of all who have touched us by their presence, by their actions and decisions, by their power to evoke the good and the best from us. We thank you for all men and women of courage who have died for their faith in you—not because they willed to die, but because they willed to live out their loyalty to whatever conclusion it might lead.

Lay upon our hearts the power of your new covenant; transform our centers of authority from the words of others to our experience of your faithful presence; free us from bondage to the many Egypts in our lives to new life in you; save us from the pseudodeaths of the spirit that rob us of vitality; reform us in the forgiving fire of your love.

Come, we pray, O God. Break into our time with your eternal love. Be to us our center of meaning, drawing together the fragments of our lives, giving shape to our faith and pattern to our hopes. Help us not to be afraid of death when it comes, but to rest in the knowledge that our dying is also part of the life you gave us. And when at last it is finished, then fulfill us and make us complete, transforming even our failures into the wholeness for which we now yearn.

But until our lives are over, help us to risk living life deeply, whether we win or lose. Quicken our pulse for justice and our desire for freedom for all your creatures. We pray in the spirit of Jesus, whose faithful action is our assurance that strength can come from helplessness, power from simplicity, and love from suffering. Amen.

7. Trust:
Death Transformed into Life

"My God, into your hands I commit my spirit!"
—*Luke 23:46*

It is now dark on Calvary, and the ground begins to shake under our feet. Those who may have turned to leave after Jesus said, "It is finished," stop as a feeling of panic rises in the crowd. Perhaps *everything* is finished. Perhaps when Jesus dies the whole world goes with him, a fitting climax for those who have crucified the Son of God.

But the last word has not yet been spoken. Jesus has looked back over his life and work, reliving those three years of his ministry as his tortured body labored in the task of dying. Yes, the past is finished. And it is clear there will be no recovery from the suffocating assault on his flesh. The present also is finished. What is not finished is what is yet to come. From somewhere deep within him, Jesus seems to get a glimpse of the future and speaks for the seventh and last time: "My God, into your hands I commit my spirit!" When he has said this, his lungs take their last breath and he dies.

Neither resignation to the end nor fulfillment of life's work is the final word for Jesus. The last word is a statement of trust—a jump into the future, a step off into the unknown, believing that God will catch him. For underneath all that agony and suffering the everlasting arms of God have been waiting to gather Jesus in and hold him to the loving heart of creation.

Some say the ground-shaking became a full-fledged earthquake after Jesus died, that even the tombs were cracked open so the saints could walk out free. Some say the curtain in the temple split right in two. Certainly a lot of people were shaken up by what happened there on Calvary, and some saw things they had never seen before, and some were changed people after that. Many went home beating their breasts in agony and in awe at what they had experienced. One unlikely person, a centurion, of all people, actually praised God, saying, "Certainly this man was innocent!" (Luke 23:47 RSV). We may wonder if he had a hard time sleeping at night after that. Or did he remember hearing Jesus ask God to forgive the executioners, and in those words find release for his soul?

Witnessing the death of Jesus puts us in touch again with the fact of our mortality. Here was a man who was born, grew up, worked, made friends, performed a ministry, and now is dead. Jesus spent his life trying to get people to change their old ways of thinking and acting, to be open to the new that is always before us. But those of us who fear death are especially afraid of the passing of time and the changes it brings. We would rather have things stay just the way they are. To us the old wine and the old ways and the old sights are always better. With Hamlet we believe it is better to "bear those ills we have than fly to others that we know not of." James Muilenburg describes our state in poignant terms:

> We are haunted again and again by the painful awareness that the shining moment passes, the day comes to an end, some silver cord of confidence is snapped, some dream dispelled, some faith shattered. The whirlgig of Time brings in its revenges. The present forever flees to the past, the future forever breaks in with relentless speed. We are forever confronted with the unexpected, the unanticipated, the new. . . . There is something profoundly disquieting and threatening in the temporality of existence. (15.226)

Nothing reminds us of our temporality more vividly than the death of another person. Even Jesus, the incarnate faithful action of God, is not spared. Time means change; the new becomes the old; the living become the dead.

To those of us who dread change, Jesus' final word rests like a blessing: "My God, into your hands I commit my spirit!" Time does march on; change is going to happen whether we like it or not; the new will appear no matter how hard we try to hang on to the old. What better place can we find to be than in God? What more certainty can there be in life or death than the knowledge that we can put ourselves in the hands of the Creator who made things the way they are? Safe in God, we can dare to embrace the oncoming new creation at work in us and around us. Within this transitory life sustained by God we are free to grow and change—to hope. The changing times are our assurance that suffering will not last forever, despair will not be endless, entrenched authority and oppressive regimes will finally die out, our worn-out bodies will not hold back the inner life of the spirit.

Our entire relationship with God is a dramatic engagement, more like a stormy love affair than a quiet time of reflection. What Jesus shows us is that the whole magnificent struggle—the successes and failures, the risks and evasions, the doubts and the affirmations—takes place in God. The Creator sustains our very energies and creativity; the spirit that infuses our bodies, our lives, our work, our love, comes from and returns to God. So even the last dreaded enemy, this end of life we call death, can be trusted as part of God's own creation.

All of us live our lives between the parentheses of beginning and end. We are born knowing we will die, and when we die, we are all that we have been since our birth. But Jesus suggests that further dimension for which we yearn. When he commits his spirit into God's hands as his last human act in this earthly life, Jesus implies that death is not the end of his spirit. Release into God is the beginning of yet a new relationship to God. We do not know its shape or form, but we can be sure this new life will be part of God's own loving faithfulness.

What Jesus says he commits to God is not his work or his self or his name or even his life. Jesus says he commits his *spirit,* a word whose counterparts in Greek, Latin, and Hebrew literally mean his very "breath." This understanding leads us back to the beginning in Genesis where we are told that God breathed into Adam's nostrils the breath of life by which that creature of dust was made a living being. Our spirit is the very breath of God in us, the power of our aliveness that makes us who we are.

We often use the word *spirit* in describing a person, meaning that essence of life that is more than the individual's body or mind, more even than the sum of those parts. *Spirit* suggests the whole person beyond any particular characteristics or traits of the physical body. In this sense, the spirit of a person is not even dependent on the individual's being alive in the flesh. We can evoke the spirit of a loved one, a friend—or of Abraham Lincoln, Martin Luther, Dietrich Bonhoeffer—and feel their power influencing and inspiring us still.

When Jesus speaks his last word from the cross, he gives the power of his aliveness to God to be put back into life again. It is this spirit, free from the confines of the body, that Jesus has told his disciples will come to them: "These things I have spoken to you, while I am still with you. But the Counselor, the Holy Spirit, whom God will send in my name, will teach you all things and bring to your remembrance all that I have said to you" (John 14:25-26 RSV). Or again, "I tell you the truth: it is to your advantage that I go away, for if I do not go away, the

Counselor will not come to you; but if I go, I will send the Holy Spirit to you" (John 16:7 RSV).

This is the spirit God breathed down at Pentecost, filling those hearts with remembrance of Jesus and those heads with the power of imaginations on fire with new life. This was the spirit that came to Paul when he was struck blind on the road to Damascus and then given back his sight that he might preach the unsearchable riches of Christ: "For by one Spirit we were all baptized into one body—Jews or Greeks, slaves or free—and all were made to drink of one Spirit" (I Cor. 12:13 RSV). This is the spirit that came to the people of faith in all ages—the martyrs, the saints, the reformers. This is the spirit that comes to us when we feel the presence and the power of Jesus' aliveness transforming our lives.

We call this Friday of crucifixion good because hidden in the suffering and the death there is the assurance of God's faithful action. The Cross proclaims, not the end of all hope, but the fulfillment of hopes and purposes that are not ours but God's. Here we find a divine purpose that takes our inhuman cruelties and our anxieties and lifts them up into a pattern of love spread across history and beyond. The words of Joseph in Egypt to his cowering brothers come back to us: "As for you, you meant to do evil against me; but God meant it for good" (Gen. 50:20 RSV). In the Cross of Christ, these words grow large with meaning. Even death can be a means by which God continues the work of transforming evil into good, death into life. "So we do not lose heart," Paul writes.

Though our outer nature is wasting away, our inner nature is being renewed every day. For this slight momentary affliction is preparing for us an eternal weight of glory beyond all comparison, because we look not to the things that are seen but to the things that are unseen; for the things that are seen are transient, but the things that are unseen are eternal. (II Cor. 4:16-18 RSV)

Many of us live our religious lives by a hope that is but a shadow—forever wondering, and always not quite sure. Certainly hope as a faint ray has often helped keep us going until the dawn of conviction arrived. But if we dwell in Jesus' last word from the cross, we may find the certainty of a hope that shall not fail. Here at the end Jesus commits his spirit to God in the conviction that God is the ground of both life and death. This act of giving one's breath of life over to God does not so much require a leap of faith as it does a release of tension and anxiety.

It is all mystery, our living and our dying. . . . As we achieve our life and death in that sense of mystery, it becomes finally a question of whether we can trust death as we trust life—as we trust loving, being loyal, being faithful, planting seeds, waiting for spring, going to sleep each night. Being able to trust is what we call "grace." (12.168)

Dwelling in Jesus opens the door for grace to work in us. We can't make it happen, but we will know when it does. Through the Cross, we are assured our trust will never be betrayed. "If we live, we live to the Lord, and if we die, we die to the Lord; so then, whether we live or whether we die, we are the Lord's. For to this end Christ died and lived again, that he might be Lord both of the dead and of the living" (Rom. 14:8-9 RSV).

The resurrection is yet to come, but the promise is here as Jesus speaks for the last time from the cross. Calvary becomes forever a part of the Passover experience. Jews celebrate the deliverance of the Israelites from Egyptian bondage—Moses leading the people through the Red Sea. Christians celebrate the deliverance of humanity from bondage to fear of death—Jesus passing from life to death to eternal life. Our Promised Land is the hand of God.

Many of us stand between the cross and the resurrection—waiting. One such person was the disciple Jesus called the Rock. What a rock! But Jesus loved and trusted Peter beyond his failures and reached out to him from beyond the separation of death. In Patricia Vought Schneider's dramatic interpretation *Peter,* we share the agony of this disciple.

> Why?
> Why did he have to die?
> Why, to pounding nails—
> to hanging on the cross, my God!—
> did he give himself to you?
> He threw his life away—
> —the rough cross-beam,
> —the pounding—
> God!—I denied I knew him,
> —as he said.
> I can't even say "forgive"—
> He is dead.

And then we hear the words of the angelic messenger:

> Do not be amazed—
> You seek Jesus of Nazareth, who was crucified.
> He is not here.

He is risen!
See the place where they laid him.
But go, tell his disciples,
—and Peter

"and——*Peter*——"

That he is going before you to Galilee.
There you will find him,
as he told you.

(23.26-27)

It is one thing to have Jesus present in our lives, for just
his being there is a blessing. But it is something else to
believe in Christ and put our trust in God enough to let it
change us, transforming even our agony and dying into
new aliveness. When Jesus said, "My God, into your
hands I commit my spirit!" the power of the resurrection
was already at work. Go tell the disciples, and Peter, and
each of us, that Jesus is in our future as well as in our past
and present. We do not need to be afraid. "If God is for us,
who is against us?" Paul asks.

Who shall separate us from the love of Christ? Shall
tribulation, or distress, or persecution, or famine, or
nakedness, or peril, or sword? . . . No, in all these things we
are more than conquerors through him who loved us. For I
am sure that neither death, nor life, nor angels, nor
principalities, nor things present, nor things to come, nor
powers, nor height, nor depth, nor anything else in all
creation, will be able to separate us from the love of God in
Christ Jesus our Lord. (Rom. 8:31*b*, 35, 37-39 RSV)

Through trust in God, even death is transformed into new
life with Jesus.

A Prayer

Lord of life and death and eternal life, we would commit our spirits into your keeping. There is so much we do not know about living and loving and working and wanting and playing and praying. So often we look around for our opportunities and find that we have missed them, and then while we lament our missed opportunities, we miss others. The days and months and years pass, and we fear the coming of winter bleakness to our lives.

Help us not to be afraid. May we find comfort in the changing of the seasons. Knowing we cannot always live in the fierce hot light of summer, may we welcome the mellow glow of autumn and then the cool embrace of winter. But may there be no brown leaves to our autumns or gray haze to our winters. Let our leaves fall when they are vibrantly full of color and our snow come down on landscapes stingingly cold and clear. May we always be alive to our changes and to the new that comes to us in time and beyond time. Give us a fervent sense of the new that always rests beneath the winter snows within us—a sense of that ever-green, ever-growing springtime of our lives that waits even now to burst forth again into bloom.

Come, O God, this day. Break into our time with your eternal presence. Be to us sun, melting the snow from our hearts; be to us rain, filling the rivers of our minds; be to us wind, blowing fresh breath of life into our spirits; be to us fire, burning our imaginations into new visions of the wonder and glory of life. We pray in the name and spirit of the risen Christ, who came and who comes again and again, assuring us that both our living and our dying are in you. Amen.

III
Breaking Out

In the beginning God created the heavens and the earth. . . . And God looked upon creation and declared it good.

—Genesis 1:1, 31

Then I saw a new heaven and a new earth; for the first heaven and the first earth had passed away, and the sea was no more. . . . And the One who sat upon the throne said, "Behold, I make all things new."

—Revelation 21:1, 5a RSV

Transforming
Human Living

From this moment forward, therefore, we view no one from a human perspective; though at one time we viewed even Christ in that way, we see him no longer from a human point of view. When a person is in Christ, that person joins the new creation; the old self is departing and, behold, the transformed self is emerging. All this comes from God, who through Christ transforms us from enemies into companions and entrusts to us the ministry of calling others to this community.

—II Corinthians 5:16-18

"Do you think he is dead?" Pilate's wife asks the centurion in John Masefield's play.

"No, lady, I don't," the soldier answers her.
"Then where is he?" she asks, uncertainty and fear peering cautiously through her words.
"Let loose in the world, lady," the centurion declares, "where neither Roman nor Jew can stop his truth."

—The Trial of Jesus

And, with the intervening centuries in mind, we might want to add, "Let loose in the world, where not even Christians with all their worldly power can stop the truth of Christ!"

That Friday of Jesus' crucifixion ended in the darkness of death. The body of Jesus was taken down tenderly from the cross and buried in the tomb offered by Joseph of Arimathea. By an amazing reversal, we have learned to call that day of tragedy and mourning Good Friday. Such a peculiar name may seem unfeeling to anyone who does not know the rest of the story—the resurrection of Jesus on the first day of the week and his appearances first to the women and then to other disciples. The resurrection altered dramatically the perspective from which Jesus' followers viewed him, his life, his teachings, his death, his cross. When we come to share that new perspective and regard Jesus no longer from a human point of view, the whole world changes. That terrible day is transformed. The Cross appears in a new light, and our lives become permeated with its strange attraction and power.

As the Roman centurion perceived, the power of the transforming Cross has been let loose in the world. The power to break out of the past, out of bondage to sin, into newness of life, has entered history. In the wake of Jesus' breaking out, human lives have been changed, human cruelties and injustices overcome, and the histories of entire peoples altered. It is no wonder that we have come to a perspective from which we call that Friday good. The tragedy remains, and with it the mystery of iniquity. But the goodness and the glory rise through the suffering and evil so that, from the height and depth of faith, we can sing:

> In the cross of Christ I glory,
> Towering o'er the wrecks of time;
> All the light of sacred story
> Gathers round its head sublime!

For those who read the Bible in faith and dwell in its story, the Cross has been a continuing source of transformation. The New Testament provides dramatic accounts of lives changed and the emerging movement of Christian faith. These stories issue a compelling summons down the centuries to us today to join the exodus from bondage and follow the God of Abraham and Sarah, of Isaac and Rebecca, of Jacob and Rachel, of Jesus Christ, toward the life of liberation and salvation.

As nowhere else, this power of transformation proclaimed in the Christian gospel comes to focus in the events swirling around the Cross. In especially poignant ways, as we have seen, the seven words spoken by Jesus from the cross convey this power to us. On Calvary, the Almighty One succumbs to crucifixion in apparent helplessness. But the seven words suggest a deeper meaning that has reverberated from century to century and from culture to culture. In the weakness of the Cross, the love of God is made manifest as the final and supreme power of the world.

God's love as it shines from the Cross provides a new perspective on the crucifixion, on human sin, on our own lives, and on the possibilities hidden within the future. The old promises of God are renewed in Jesus Christ. What appears from a human point of view as the death of a good person becomes in transformed perspective the pinnacle of God's work of redemption.

Among the most moving testimonies in the Christian story to the transforming power of the Cross is the life of Saul of Tarsus, who became Paul, the Apostle to the Gentiles. After gaining notoriety as a relentless persecutor of Christians, Saul met the risen Christ on the road to Damascus. The entire meaning and direction of his life were changed by that encounter. And the world has never recovered from the energy, the eloquence, and the sheer force of this transformation. Paul wrote much of our New Testament in letters struck off in the heat of passionate commitment, so strong are they that the very language in which we express our faith is indelibly marked by his genius: "I have been crucified with Christ; it is no longer I who live, but Christ who lives in me; and the life I now live in the flesh I live by faith in the Son of God, who loved me and gave himself for me" (Gal. 2:20 RSV). As Paul experienced vividly in his own life, human living can be transformed when the crucified Christ lives in us. The eyes of our understanding are opened. Our hearts are enlightened. We see a new world. We live a new life.

The power of the Cross has entered the lives of millions more. It has entered our lives and yours. For some, the entry of Christ into their lives has been marked by deep upheaval, by spiritual thunder and lightning. For others, that entry has been more quiet, a gradual process developed through the supporting love of parents and Christian community, through words of encouragement in the face of disappointment, through the understanding presence of friends as we have confronted grief, or through service and action as we met Jesus in human need and social injustice. God's grace has a thousand secret stratagems as surely as it can be brazen and noisy, or appear in the towering destinies of nations.

Augustine of Hippo heard a chance voice in a garden and broke out of a sensuous life-style in the decadent Roman Empire to become a follower of Christ. Faith transformed him. He became a bishop in North Africa and wrote treatises that shaped Christianity for a thousand years.

Francis of Assisi broke out of a middle-class affluence that had become meaningless to him. Under the transforming power of the Cross, Francis lived a life of simple faith and devoted service to the poor. His example was a silent, devastating judgment upon churchly wealth and ecclesiastical ostentation in the thirteenth century, and it remains so today. Few humans have inspired more persons to humane living than Francis and his followers.

Martin Luther, dutiful and learned monk, found himself transformed by the insight that it is faith in Jesus Christ and not good works that is at the heart of the gospel. So empowered, he led the Protestant Reformation and laid the foundations for a renewal of Christian faith that sent men and women on courageous missions around the globe to proclaim the message of the crucified and risen Lord.

John Newton ran a British slave ship between Africa and the slave marts of America in the early nineteenth century. He led worship on the main deck for the crew while the cries of blacks doomed to slavery welled up from below. But Newton came to hate that life. Transformed by the love of Christ suffering on the cross, he rejected slave-running and became a minister. For his epitaph he wrote this moving testimony:

JOHN NEWTON, Clerk,
Once an infidel and Libertine,
A servant of slaves in Africa,
Was, by the rich mercy of our Lord and Saviour

JESUS CHRIST
Preserved, restored, pardoned,
And appointed to preach the Faith
He had long laboured to destroy.

(22.175)

Beginning with the raw stuff of this world's sorrows—treachery, injustice, hatred, sensuality, greed, suffering, death—the Cross transforms them all. Persons are changed as they join the group on Calvary. History takes a new turning on that hill, at that point in time and space. Deathless deeds are done; changed lives are lived in the name and power of the One who dies there.

And the work of transformation goes on in our own time. Michael Polanyi, a brilliant scientist who found home and faith in England after being forced to flee Hitler's Germany, speaks of "dwelling in" and "breaking out":

The indwelling of the Christian worshipper is therefore a continued attempt at breaking out, at casting off the condition of man even while humbly acknowledging its inescapability. . . . Christian worship sustains, as it were, an eternal, never to be consummated hunch: a heuristic vision which is accepted for the sake of its unresolvable tension. It is like an obsession with a problem known to be insoluble, which yet follows, against reason, unswervingly, the heuristic command: "Look at the unknown!" Christianity sedulously fosters, and in a sense permanently satisfies, man's craving for mental dissatisfaction by offering him the comfort of a crucified God. (19.198-99)

How does the work of the transforming Cross occur in our lives? How can we so dwell in our faith that we are enabled to break out from our old ways into new awareness and new action? By not letting our hearts become hardened against change, by desiring transformation, by imagining ourselves living the abundant life proclaimed in the Gospels. This means listening to Jesus and to the entire Christian story, not just with our ears to get the story accurately, not just with our minds to understand it intellectually, but listening with our whole selves, with heart and soul and mind and strength, until we hear in this story the story of our own life.

Then we live through the story. Who of us has not mocked someone? Which of us has not sided with injustice to protect our own interests, joined the crowd in what we knew to be wrong, slept comfortably while another endured anguish? Who of us has not been compelled to watch helplessly while someone we loved died, or felt the sting of failure as the cause to which we were loyal went down to defeat? By desiring it, by imagining it, we can dwell in all the characters of the Passion story. If we can become each person in turn and discover ourselves before the Cross of Christ, then it becomes possible for us to be transformed by its power. When the curtain of the temple has been torn in two and Jesus has breathed his last, we may then be able to confess with the Roman centurion, "Truly this man was a son of God!" (Mark 15:39 RSV).

Once we have seen Jesus Christ on the cross through eyes of faith, things can never be the same for us again. The newness that Israel saw and proclaimed in the activity of the covenant God, the newness that Christians discover and witness to in the faithful action in Jesus

Christ, becomes our own new life. We are being transformed.

At times the everydayness of our location will deaden our remembrance of that story. Becoming inundated by the ordinary, we may forget who we are as Christians. Sometimes we feel we are drowning in a sea of despair and determinism. But we know help is near. Each of us lives in a sustaining atmosphere of unmerited services and grace—from family and friends, from those with whom we work and chance contacts in the community, and from many more whose ministrations we perceive only in that the milk is delivered and the groceries are on the market shelf. The story of Christian faith enables us to discover ourselves engulfed, not in despair, but rather in the faithful love of God. The means for this discovery may be as close as the daily newspaper, the next street-corner encounter, our church, or our Bible. The story of God's love has many vehicles, many guises.

Christians do not live at sunset but at dawn, toward an ever-emerging future of hope that has the strange shape of a cross. "There is a group of Protestant Christian monks in France," we are told, "which has as part of its confession and dedication the phrase: do not be afraid to precede the dawn" (11.110). The church of Jesus Christ, when true to the God who is never stationary, has moved toward the dawn of ecumenical relations, toward a renewed sense of mission *in* the world, toward a new day of racial equality and social justice. But there are new dawns to be anticipated, new transformations of human history that will be as momentous as any remembered in the great stories of our faith. As Christians, we participate in this newness of continuing creation as we ourselves are re-created.

The Bible provides the most enduring resource of Christian faith for that enlightenment which transforms the heart. From beginning to end it speaks of God, the Faithful One, at work creating, re-creating, making all things new. Even the good creation depicted in Genesis is not a static perfection, but is a creation in progress toward greater fulfillment. At the end of the Bible, in the book of Revelation, God is disclosed as engaged in new creation. Heaven and earth—human life, the world of history, the natural order—are being reshaped toward an unfolding future. God is always on the move, ever going before us in cloud and fire, leading us on a continuing exodus out of bondage with a promise ever old toward liberation ever new.

Christian faith, drawing on the biblical story, proclaims that the future of God, in continuity with the promises of the covenant, is filled with newness and with hope. Jürgen Moltmann, emphasizing the promise at the heart of the gospel, writes: "From first to last, and not merely in the epilogue, Christianity is eschatology, is hope, forward looking and forward moving, and therefore also revolutionizing and transforming the present" (14.16).

If we can lift our vision to the Cross, we will discover around us a world filled with sin, with pain, with injustice, with despair, in need of our involvement and concern. But we will also discover a world filled with possibilities of change, of repentance, of new life. God is in our midst, lifted up on every cross of human suffering, summoning us to live in faith and hope and love. As we dwell in our faith and remember the mighty acts of God among the

Hebrews and in Jesus Christ, we are empowered to break out of the ordinary and into the newness of life promised in the gospel.

There are three crosses on Golgotha. Two were and remain the terrible instruments of Roman execution. But the third is the transforming Cross of God.

Bibliography

1. Baillie, D. M. *God Was in Christ*. New York: Charles Scribner's Sons, 1948.
2. Baillie, John. *Invitation to Pilgrimage*. New York: Charles Scribner's Sons, 1942.
3. Berryhill, Elizabeth G. "Spiritual Aspects of Twentieth-Century American Drama." Lecture delivered at the San Francisco Theological Seminary, 20 February 1961, San Anselmo, California.
4. Berryhill, Helen. "Mea Culpa." In *Oh, I See*. San Mateo, 1974.
5. Bonhoeffer, Dietrich. *Letters and Papers from Prison*. The enlarged edition edited by Eberhard Bethge. New York: The Macmillan Co., 1953.
6. Buechner, Frederick. *Wishful Thinking: A Theological ABC*. New York: Harper & Row, 1973.
7. Dinsmore, Charles Allen. *Atonement in Literature and Life*. Boston: Houghton, Mifflin & Co., 1906.
8. "I'll Go On Sweeping the Corridor." Interview. London: British Broadcasting Corporation, no date.

9. Masefield, John. *The Trial of Jesus.* New York: The Macmillan Co., 1925.

10. May, Rollo. *Love and Will.* New York: W. W. Norton & Co., 1969.

11. McCoy, Charles S., and Neely D. McCarter. *The Gospel on Campus: Rediscovering Evangelism in the Academic Community.* Richmond: John Knox Press, 1959

12. McCoy, Marjorie Casebier. *To Die With Style!* Nashville: Abingdon, 1974.

13. Moltmann, Jürgen. "The Crucified God." In *Theology Today,* April 1974.

14. ———. *Theology of Hope: On the Ground and the Implications of a Christian Eschatology.* Translated by James W. Leitch. New York: Harper & Row, 1967.

15. Muilenburg, James. "The Biblical View of Time." In *Harvard Theological Review,* October 1961.

16. Niebuhr, H. Richard. *The Meaning of Revelation.* New York: The Macmillan Co., 1941.

17. Paton, Alan. *Cry, the Beloved Country.* New York: Charles Scribner's Sons, 1948.

18. ———. "In Memoriam: Albert Luthuli." In *Christianity and Crisis,* 18 September 1967.

19. Polanyi, Michael. *Personal Knowledge: Towards a Post-Critical Philosophy.* Chicago: University of Chicago Press, 1958.

20. Rilke, Rainer Maria. *Letters to a Young Poet.* New York: W. W. Norton & Co., 1934.

21. Sayers, Dorothy L. *The Man Born to Be King: A Play-Cycle on the Life of Our Lord and Saviour Jesus Christ.* New York: Harper & Brothers, 1943.

22. Scherer, Paul. *Facts That Undergird Life.* New York: Harper & Brothers, 1938.

23. Schneider, Patricia Vought. *Peter.* A one-act play with music by Louis Born. Boston: Walter H. Baker Co., 1971.

24. Thurman, Howard. *Disciplines of the Spirit.* New York: Harper & Row, 1963.

25. Tournier, Paul. *Guilt and Grace, A Psychological Study.* Translated by Arthur W. Heathcote *et al.* New York: Harper & Row, 1962.
26. Wiesel, Eli. *Night.* New York: Bard Avon Books, 1972.
27. Wilder, Thornton. *The Angel That Troubled the Waters, and Other Plays.* New York: Coward-McCann, 1928.
28. Wink, Walter. *The Bible in Human Transformation: Toward a New Paradigm for Biblical Study.* Philadelphia: Fortress Press, 1973.
29. Wolfe, Thomas. *Look Homeward, Angel.* New York: Charles Scribner's Sons, 1929.